T0117141

POETIC EXPERIENCES

OF

Life

James H. Brown II

authorHOUSE®

AuthorHouse™
1663 Liberty Drive
Bloomington, IN 47403
www.authorhouse.com
Phone: 1-800-839-8640

Published by AuthorHouse   03/09/2012

ISBN: 978-1-4685-6243-9 (sc)

First and foremost, I would like to thank God for giving me the ability and confidence to compose this book unto his people. Being the Captain of my ship and the Master of my life. He has given me so much as well as allowing me to go through so much to make me who I am. I feel that this is only the tip of the iceberg for the best is yet to come.

Next I would like to thank my wife Angela for always believing in me and knowing that I can do all things through Christ who guide and strengthens me. Words along can't merely express the channels in which she has always motivated me thus prompting me to continue to excel in order to be the best that I can be.

Next I would like to thank my children Kabrina, Kensley, Kabretta, Carriea and Shandreika for being inspirational and the motivation and the continued love and support not to mention the earthly desires that I have to find a way to provide for them especially my Grandkids La'Bria Tierra Childs(Genius), Madison Morrahia and Naizel Pounds.

I could finish this book thanking all of the numerous people that has helped and inspired me in one way or another but I know that you are anxious to get to this material.

> **If I can change one person life with what I write or say, I will have chartered the course of their entire generation . . .**
> **James H. Brown**

This book is volume I which is a small sample of an upcoming series. It is designed to have a reading audience ranging from 8 to 80 and beyond. Consisting of 150 poems in 8 different categories from drug intervention to spiritual reality along with a lot of other different projects, essays and theories are among the things that you will enjoy.

May you continually be blessed with the contents of this book.

Contents

Chapter I- Drug Intervention

1. The Duel 1
2. Mr. Crack 2
3. Mrs. Meth 4
4. Holocaust 6
5. No Friend of Mine 7
6. The Dynamic Illusion 8
7. Cracktown 9
8. Vain Beauty 10
9. Desperado 11

Chapter II –Spiritual Reality

10. If Jesus Had Ran Away 12
11. The Merciful Messiah 14
12. Crucified 15
13. Sacrifice 16
14. Heaven 17
15. Hell 18
16. Here I am 19
17. Resurrection 20
18. Awesome 21
19. Host 23

20. Decide..24
21. Who am I? 25
22. Me 27

Chapter III- Education and Inspiration

23. School's Tools....................................29
24. Smart..30
25. Our Immaculate mind 31
26. Continuation 32
27. Choose 33
28. Go Right or Be Left 35
29. You Better Not Quit 37
30. Fool..38
31. Stormy 39
32. Blackman...40
33. Black Woman......................................42

Chapter IV- The Blacks History

34. Homeland 44
35. Voyage..45
36. Oppressed...46
37. Freeman 48
38. Amistad 49
39. Harriett Tubman................................51
40. The Blacks History.............................53
41. Garrett A. Morgan 55
42. Howard University 57
43. Thank You Dr. King............................58
44. Coretta 60
45. The American pride 62

Chapter V– Mighty Katrina

46. Katrina 63
47. Mighty Katrina 65
48. Misery 67
49. Spared 69
50. Banished 70
51. Home 72
52. I AM 74

Chapter VI– The Twin Towers

53. God 75
54. Look out 76
55. 911 78
56. American 79
57. Wanted 81
58. Doomed 82
59. Fear 83
60. Angels Around 84
61. Where 85
62. Save Me 86
63. The Heroes 87
64. Crash 88
65. Maintain 89
66. Gone 90
67. My Job 91
68. Help 92
69. Survival 93
70. Men of Honor 94
71. Your Hero 96
72. My Hero 98

Chapter VII —Miscellaneous

73. Golden memories 100
74. Raw Deal 101
75. Remember 103
76. True Champion 105
77. Seventy-Six 107
78. Perhaps 109
79. A Great Man 111
80. A Better Macon 113
81. T-Bo Greene *114*
82. The Man 116
83. Time 117
84. Home 119
85. Me 120
86. The Champ 122
87. Winner 123
88. Grace 124
89. Host 125
90. An Angel 126
91. Don't Worry 127
92. Happy Birthday Jesus 128
93. A Miracle 129
94. Heaven 130
95. My Love 131
96. Bonded 132
97. Devotion 133
98. Change 135
99. Anti-Drug Festival 2005 136
100. Ray Hagin 137
101. Elvis 139
102. Saint Paul 140
103. Hallelujah 143

104. Tomorrow 144
105. Love 145
106. Mighty Mother... 146
107. Free Father 147
108. Guardian... 149
109. The Egg theory 151
110. Sacred Center 153
111. A Change 155
112. Angela 157
113. Blackman Ineffectual Annihilation.................. 159
114. Reality 162
115. Arisen... 164
116. Racist 166
117. Profound Love.. 167
118. Greatest Love... 168
119. Next.. 170
120. Extra Ordinary People 171
121. Victorious... 173
122. Heavy.. 174
123. Madness.. 175
124. Help 177
125. Happy Anniversary.. 178
126. Hall of Famer 179
127. Homelessness.. 181
128. Living.. 182
129. Commitment.. 184
130. Confession.. 185
131. Happy Birthday Jarvis 187
132. Mother Dear 188
133. Big Cuz... 190
134. Color Blind 192
135. Face to Face 194
136. Harm's Way... 195

137. Angel.. 196

138. You 197

139. God Almighty.. 198

140. Who am I? 199

141. Revelation 201

142. I Believe 203

143. Love 204

144. Drug-Free 205

145. Life 206

146. The Lord.. 207

147. Mother.. 208

148. Mattie... 210

149. Our Momma.. 211

The Duel

Mr. Crack and Mrs. Meth are battling for your
precious soul.
They both already destroyed countless lives untold.
They both are only weapons that Satan has chosen to use.
Their sole purpose is to annihilate you, so please
don't be confused.
Mr. Crack is bragging that he is leading the way.
Mrs. Meth proudly proclaims that she will lead one day.
She claims that Mr. Crack is too expensive and very
hard to get.
But she can be made in a lab or a pit.
Whether you are Black, White, young or old they really
don't care.
They are battling for your soul so you better be aware.

Mr. Crack

Hello everybody, my name is Mr. Crack.
Yall tried to destroy me but guess what? I'm back.
Now I got it going on and it's ever so strong!
I've made it even harder for you to leave me alone.
You might try to leave me; maybe you'll stay a day or two.
That's when I'll tell your poor brains exactly what to do.
You can run while you're awake but I'll catch you in
your sleep.
I'll make an old man roam and a new born baby weep.
I don't care who I get you may even think that you're bad.
When you fall in my deadly trap, you'll know that you've
been had.
I'll make you neglect your rent, I'll tell you to
forget your bills.
When you think about my scent I will certainly
make you steal.
You'll forget about your kids, you won't think
about the strife.
Your valuables you'll start to bid and you'll soon
give up on life.
I'm telling you I don't play no matter what you say.
I'll even destroy my dealers if they let me have my way.

My name is Crack and I know that I am bad!
My only real purpose is to destroy you and make you sad.
Get mad!!! I don't care, try me if you dare. I'll have it so
you won't have anything to wear.
No matter how much money you got, I'll get it all in time.
If you do too much of me I will cause you to go blind.
If that's not enough I can tell you even more.
I've made billions of people throw their life out the door.
So if you think that you are smart, I'll tell you what to do.
I am going to do my part so don't you touch me or
you're through.
There is no way to win my friend, it's a dead end!

Mrs. Meth

All drugs are dangerous but I am the best!
My name is Crystal, they call me Meth.
I entertained Hitler so I'm not new to this game.
To meddle with me you must be insane.
I'm cooked in the home or anywhere,
With my deadly fume I contaminate the air.
My ingredients are dangerous, some you won't believe.
I am more deadly than your simple mind can conceive.
Clorox, sulfur, gasoline, red lye, and my ingredients alone
will make you die.
There's a strong chance that I might even explode, and
scatter your home all over the road.
I'll destroy your teeth and deteriorate your skin.
There is absolutely no way that you can possibly win.
I'll take a girl, mesmerize her world and make her look like
a poor lost squirrel.
I'll take a baby and make it cry all day then make the
Mother throw it away.
I'll make a man act like a boy and make his teal
his child's only toy,
I'll make a teacher forget how to teach; I'll make a
Preacher kill before he preaches.

I'll entrap your soul and never set you free.

I'll make you as miserable as you can possibly be.

I don't care about you, and I never will. I want your soul
and all you have to give.

I'm the most deadly drug that you have ever seen.

I will break up your home and destroy all your dreams.

Please believe what you have just heard because
it is all true.

All you got to do is try me once and I bet that
you'll be through.

Yes, I will control your life one day at a time and you'll
have no idea that you'll slowly be dying.

Crystal Methamphanine, yeah that's me, if you're bad try
me once and I bet that you will see.

That I am your worst nightmare!

Holocaust

Let's build an alliance to serve one cause.
Together we can make the whole world lost.
Together we are deadly and can't be beat.
Our only purpose is to destroy and defeat.
Mr. Crack and Mrs. Meth hand in hand.
Claiming victims all over the land.
Blacks, Whites or Asians, young and old.
Let's destroy their lives and claim their soul.
Let's put more attention on the young boys and girls.
By getting them now, we can conquer the world.
By the time that they realize that the war on us is lost.
We would have started a drug Holocaust!

No Friend of Mine

I really don't think that you are a friend of mine.
If you were I doubt that you would cause me to be blind.
Blind to reality in a different world that I have
never seen before.
Locked within a deadly twirl and can't find the door.
It all started when you suggested that we have some fun.
I never thought that you were trying to convert
me into a bum.
To lose in life is not something that a friend would
help you do!
You knew at first that if I started my life would be through.

You are no friend of mine!

The Dynamic Illusion

The dynamic illusion causes constant confusions.
It always alters your mind.
It promotes neglect and disrespect and undoubtly wastes
your time.
To indulge in something to bring you down is really not
too smart.
Upon addiction it makes you a clown and set you far apart.
Apart from the world to be alone in the corners
of your mind.
Is really not where you belong and you're definitely
wasting your time.

It's only an illusion

Cracktown

All around the world the towns are the same.
There are countless of souls that crack has claimed.
There are millions of lives that are lost every day.
Crime increases as crack leads the way.
It's rapidly spreading from town to town.
Upon its arrival the city goes down.
Businesses shut down and boards go up.
The population decreases as the city corrupts.
There are dilapidated houses on every street.
They are the places where the dealers and users meet.
You must be careful everywhere you go.
You may be the next victim you'll never know.
Crack creatures have evolved everywhere.
For your sacred life, they don't even care.
Cracktown, USA
The love of money has made it this way.
Cracktown, USA
What a dangerous place in which we stay.

Vain Beauty

Endowed in beauty, ultimately unique.

Addicted on cocaine and headed for defeat.

Led unaware down crack's deadly road.

Undoubtly she doesn't care as her beauty starts to mold.

Now she's sinking in sorrow and drowning in despair.

She's not thinking about tomorrow, as for today she's unaware.

Her beauty is in vain.

My what a shame!

All because she's addicted to cocaine.

Desperado

A ruthless criminal out with a gun.
His intentions are to spoil everybody's fun.
He doesn't care who his victims will be.
He is going after their valuables you see.
He is really a good guy needing a hug.
But living a high and strung out on drugs.
Besides from a gun he carries a knife.
He is always prepared to take someone's life.

If Jesus Had Ran Away

What if Jesus Had ran away?
Let us examine that very first day.
Then we will end with that dreadful night to show us saints
his ultimate plight.
Before he had came if he had ran away,
No North Star would have shined through the day.
No wise men would come through the night.
His mother and father would have never taken flight.
If Jesus had simply ran away would John have lived to
preach one day?
For John was barren in his mother's womb, could that have
been his silent tomb?
What if Jesus had ran away when John was baptizing in
full array?
Thus he had never seen Jesus come, could his work have
ever been done?
What if Jesus had ran away and didn't go to the desert not
one single day.
And nothing descended from heave above,
In which God did openly express his love.
What if Jesus had ran away without ever teaching what
God had to say.

What would we do? Who would we know?
What could we say? Where would we go?
If Jesus had never died on the cross, the whole world
would still be lost.
He wouldn't have had Hell's keys in His hand.
Then Satan would have conquered the entire land.
If Jesus had chosen to run away.
There wouldn't be nothing that we could say!
There wouldn't be nothing that we could do!
There would be no me; and there would be no you!

The Merciful Messiah

The merciful Messiah is who I am.
I am of God, I am the lamb.
I am your Savior; I am your King.
I can do anything!
I can go through the mountain.
I can walk on the seas.
I can speak to the wind and control the bees.
I can make the blind see I can make the lame walk.
I can cure all diseases and make the dumb talk.
But there is one thing that I cannot do!
That's take your heart just to save you.
I wake you up each and every day.
Then make sure that blessings always come your way.
I put you to be every single night.
And make sure that everything is always alright.
I gave you my life to follow me.
I want to make you happy; I want to make you free.
You have my mercy, you have my love.
You have more compassion than you can ever dream of.
So give me your heart and follow me.
On Judgment day, where will you be?

Crucified

I was hung on the cross.

To save your soul for it was lost.

If I had not done what I did.

From your sins you could never be rid.

It was written before your time.

As a sacrifice to put you back in line.

In line with God to clean your heart.

To give man-kind a brand new start.

So take my hand and walk with me.

Accept salvation so you can be free.

Free from all the sins of the world.

For your soul is more precious than pearls.

It doesn't matter what your situation maybe.

Look what the world did to me.

Pilate let the people have their say.

They chose Barbabas a thief, and let him got away!

It was said and done so all is well.

I hung on the cross to save you from Hell.

Sacrifice

You were sacrificed to give us life.

You endured too much pain and strife.

You are the peace that gives us understanding.

To understand you is to know that you loved us first.

To know you is to love you in return.

To love you is to follow you.

For you showed us just how much you love us by doing
what you did.

By loving you we can achieve all things.

We must have the love for you that you have for us.

Which is unconditional love.

May we judge not and be without doubt that you carried it
all to the cross.

Just for us!

Heaven

I can only imagine what Heaven is like.

I heard that it's a breathtaking sight.

I know that seeing it will take your breath away.

You'll stand there speechless with no words to say.

I can only imagine the solid gold streets.

And the river of milk and honey where everyone meet.

There will be no sorrow; there will be no pain.

There will be no cripple; there will be no lame.

There will be no sickness; there will be no death.

There will only be joy with an abundance of wealth.

I can only imagine many mansions in a house.

Where the cat will love and get along with the mouse.

We don't have to imagine, just live the right way.

Then we will get to see God's Heaven one day.

We will see the Throne sitting behind a sea of glass.

Then we will be able to say that we are free at last.

Hell

I left the cross to go down below.
I went to Hell and opened the door.
I stepped inside and looked around.
Fire was blazing and souls were bound.
All I could smell was burning flesh.
Everyone there had failed the test.
From my presence demons had to flee.
For the Glory of god was all around me.
Lost souls were begging me to set them free.
But it was written so it must be.
What a dreadful place hell is below.
Please my child try not to go!
Condition your mind and clean your heart.
The decision is yours so you better be smart.
I made Satan get on his knees.
Before I left I took the keys.
Hell has room for many, many more.
The conditions are horrible so try not to go.

Here I am

Her I am, I came back for you.
Now that I am here what will you do?
Now that I am back, get your life right.
You have a chance to get on track.
I went down and took the keys of Hell.
We all know that is where Satan dwells.
He has no power over you or me.
If you open your eyes it's easy to see.
His job is to deceive you and tell you a lie.
His purpose is to mislead you and steal your
soul when you die.
You are never alone; I am always fighting for you.
The Holy Spirit always tells you what to do.
All you got to do is to call on my name.
Together we will put that old serpent to shame.
So here I am just waiting for you.
I want to make your life brand new.
Get saved today . . .

Resurrection

After three days in He'll, they rolled back the stone.
They looked inside, my body was gone.
There were angels standing where I had been.
They told Mary and Martha that I had come back again.
The saints were happy to see my face.
So they ran to tell the others of God's glorious grace.
Some did not believe what they were told.
Thomas stuck his finger straight through the hole.
I had holes in my hand and holes in my feet.
My total ascension was not yet complete.
Everyone was speechless for it was hard to believe.
Resurrection from death was hard to conceive.
It strengthened their Faith in Almighty God.
This made it easier to do their part.
So you must believe that he is coming back again.
Ready or not it will be the end.

Awesome

We all try to wonder what God is like.
But our minds can't conceive His glorious might.
Our ears can't adhere to his harmonious sound.
So we will never know when he comes around.
Our eyes can never see the things that he do.
He can take the old and refurbish it new.
You see, God is like the Ocean, vast, deep and wide.
We can never see to the other side.
God is like the wind with its ever-changing blow.
It can soothe your body or cause you to woe.
God is like the fire that can't be quenched, consuming
entirely in a synch.
God is like the earth with its elements in his hand.
Everything that exists is under his command.
So there is something that you should know.
It's that God sees everywhere that you go.
God sees everything that you do.
He is always standing right there to pull you through.
Our ways are not his and his is not our, He is the
undeniable Infinite power.
So it's smart to fear God in everything that you do.
Get wisdom, knowledge and understanding too.

Being tried by the fire and sliced by the sword,
You have a chance to reap the reward.
So it doesn't matter what you say or do. God's vibrant
word is holy and true.
You must read the word and do what is say, while giving
him the highest praises each and every day.
Oh what an awesome God we serve.

Host

I am your host, let me in.
You can't win against sin.
All by yourself, you won't prevail.
You'll only send yourself to hell.
I am here for you to make you strong.
I'll teach you how to leave sins alone.
Just do the things that I tell you to do.
Then watch your life become brand new.
You have powers that you do not know.
Power to make the Devil go.
Go back to Hell from which He came.
Your soul is at stake so this is no game.
How long must I wait?
What are you going to do?
When Jesus comes back you will be through.

Decide

This is my purpose; what is your plan?

I am of God; you are of man.

I came to earth just for you.

My job is to help pull you through.

I have powers that you do not know.

Where I am, I want you to go.

It's not my Father will that any should perish.

But you are the ones that he does cherish.

For righteousness I died on the cross.

Because your souls were forever lost.

That was the only way that I could wash away your sins.

I am the key to let you in.

So now everything is up to you.

You can still do what you want to do.

You have your life and you have you heart.

You can choose Satan or you can choose God.

Whatever you decide to do, you did it to yourself.

If you don't make it to Heaven you can't
blame anyone else.

The decision is yours . . .

Who am I?

Who am I? Who wants to know?
You wouldn't believe me if I told you so.
You won't believe that I sit on high.
I control the earth from the infinite sky.
Who am I? Who wants to know?
You wouldn't believe me if I told you so.
You won't believe that I sit on high.
I control the earth from the infinite sky.
You don't believe that I know everything.
Even the weather before the season brings.
You won't believe that I raised the dead.
And by a little boys lunch 5000 people were fed.
You won't believe that I turned water into wine and gave
sight to some people who were born blind.
Who am I? Do you really want to know?
Listen closely and I will tell you so.
Close your eyes and open your mind, picture the ocean
that so divine.
Picture the sand along the shore, now come to me I have
open the door.
For I am the ocean, vast deep and wide, you don't want to
see the other side.

You will never know nor will you ever understand.
That infinite wisdom is too mighty for man.
I am the way, the truth and the light. Everything that I do is honorable and right.
I made the beast with eyes to and fro, just to see you anywhere you go.
I am that I Am, I am the Lamb, I am the Father of Abraham.
Ears can never hear nor can eyes ever see the glorious power inside of me.
Who am I? Who wants to know? If you are sure I will tell you so.
I AM all that I appear to be, I AM that I AM.

Me

God placed me upon this Earth.
I had no idea as to what I was worth.
Within me there is a light that shines so bright.
That it guides my way through the dark, cold night.
As I adventure within this long lost world.
I find that my gift is like a pearl.
Within an oyster and as precious as can be.
Sent down from Heaven and appointed unto me.
The words that I write can set soul free. Thus making
mankind hunger for me.
Words that tantalizes ones thoughts and mesmerizes
one's mind.
Setting the captive free and leading the blind.
I remember the things that I use to do.
How I went through life not knowing who.
Who I was or from whence I came.
Always looking for someone on who to blame.
Much was said and much was done.
Through it all a lesson was learned.
He lives in me and me in He, His glorious light shines
inside of me.
My path was laid before I came, even before I had a name.

The victory had already been won even before I was born.
God made the Earth and God made the sea. God put his
spirit inside of me.
So I thank you Father for who I am, and keep me close to
Jesus the Lamb.
I am a shining light for all to see.
I am of God for He lives in me.

School's Tools

There once lived a little boy that really loved school.
Because of his dedication to school, His friends all thought
that he was a fool.
He always took notes and studied real hard.
He had all A's on his report card.
It all started after graduation day.
They all grew up and they all moved away.
Ten years later they were forced to meet.
At the class reunion was the entire fleet.
They all laughed at how they all had failed.
The ones that were absent were still in jail.
There was one more to explain about his strife
His love for his books they thought he had no life. But
they were all wrong for he had come a long way. His love
for his books had helped him to say
You were the fools that didn't like school. I tried to tell
you that books were a tool
I made my first million years ago, that's because I built a
bookstore
Now I have bookstores all over the land and millions are
falling right in my hand.
So you tell me who was the fool?
It really paid me to learn in school.

Smart

Reading is the greatest thing to do.
You'll discover things that you never knew.
You can go places that no one goes.
You can learn things that no one knows.
You can climb the mountains.
You can swim the seas.
You can soar with eagles or swarm with bees.
Elevating your mind to tremendous heights.
Seeking wisdom and knowledge with all of your might.
For knowledge is power!
It will help you to win!
Reading will teach you where to begin.
So read your mind to a brighter day.
If you don't your mind will decay.

Our Immaculate mind

The mind is the most mysterious product that was
given to modern man.
Its channels are so remarkable that we cannot understand.
With its unforgettable memory monitoring every thought.
Even beneath the victory of yesterday in which it
dreadfully fought.
It ventures while we're asleep and wonders
when we're awake.
It never reaches its peak thus adventures it undertakes.
It must be revealed that our mind is ours to use.
It can't be neglected or us it will abuse.
So let's study it entirely and include it in our race.
To achieve our goal of excellence because it's too
valuable to waste.

The mind is a terrible thing to waste.

Continuation

We were born as individuals with our own distinctive
personalities.
In this world we must submit to mistakes and technicalities.
So as you venture through life you will undoubtly be told.
That there are certain things that are beyond your control.
So it doesn't matter how you feel.
Sometimes your situation won't seem real.
Always keep in mind that time doesn't yield.
For life must go on.
It doesn't matter what you say when things don't
sometimes go your way.
Always look forward to another day.
For life must go on.
You may find that there are things that you'd like to do.
No matter how you try, you can't see them through.
You must be content with what pleases you.
For Life must go on.
If you try hard you certainly will win, considering you're
conquering life only then.
Just remember that you maybe down again.
For Life will go on.

Choose

Today's choices are tomorrow's realities is a saying
that is so true.
You are in control of your own life so your
future is up to you.
If you can dream it you can achieve it is
what they always say.
Time doesn't stop and wait for no one
so you must start today.
Education is the key to your success for
anything that you want to do.
You must always do your best nothing less
will pull you through.
It's always best to be # 1 in the race.
Number 2 is always second place.
You can never win if you never try.
You can soar like an eagle ever so high.
Gliding high in the sky with the wind beneath your wings.
Making sounds more beautiful than any bird can ever sing.
Your destiny is in your hands so it's all left up to you.

You must make the right choices or you definitely
will be through.
Reality will come tomorrow from the choices
that we make today.
So please don't be a failure by throwing your life away.

Make the right choices today.

Go Right or Be Left

Go right or be left is the phase for today.
You can't do both so you must go one way.
Neither has anything to do with the other.
They are as different as a Father and a Mother.
You can go right and be the best that you can be.
You can be successful, living happy and free.
Having the best of things in all aspects of life.
Having risen above confusion, poverty and strife.
Always being content in everything that you do.
Getting a good education which is looking out for you.
Or you can choose to be left which is totally up to you.
No one can every make you learn anything
if you don't want to.
No one will ever make you go anywhere you
don't want to go.
No one can ever teach you things that you
do not want to know.
Being left is not good for you will find yourself behind.
You may live a life of poverty and always be in a bind.

Go right or be left.
What are you going to do?
This is a step that you must take.
So the choice is up to you.

Do the right thing . . . .

You Better Not Quit

You better not quit, listen to what I say.
Although it may get harder with each passing day.
It may get to a point where you know you can't win.
If you're knocked down get up again.
If the winning seems like it's just too hard.
You have some help just call on God.
There is nothing that we can do on our own.
Where we are weak he makes us strong.
You may get dog tired and can't help but to rest.
You better keep on fighting at your very best.
If the fight gets you down a bit, rest if you must but you
better not quit.
Winners are in a class all by themselves, they are
unlike anyone else.
Victory starts in their heart; you can see it in their eyes.
When they win it's no surprise.
Losers are strange they don't expect to win.
It's not in their heart where it should begin.
It is possible to win although you may lose.
Success doesn't always follow the rules.
It has been proven that life will get you down a bit.
But it's all part of living so you better not quit.

Fool

Sometimes people just don't know.
What is right or which way to go.
They live each day like they just don't care.
Not realizing that their life is rare.
The world is too serious to live that way.
It's a blessing to wake up every day.
Education is something that should be important to you.
You'll definitely need knowledge to pull you through.
In school it's available every day.
You have the greatest teachers, don't throw it away.
Being blind to the world and still expecting the best.
Neglecting your education and settling for less.
Knowledge is power, one day you will see.
While you are in school be the best that you can be.
So please don't make a fool of yourself.
Then blame your failure on someone else.

Stormy

The storm is passing over; I can finally see the clouds.
The rain was pouring and the thunder was so loud.
It was so dark that I couldn't see my hand in
front of my face.
I ne4ver would have made it if it wasn't for God's grace.
I never would have made it because I didn't
know what to do.
Not once was I afraid for I know that God would pull me
through.
I knew that it was just a test to help me be strong.
To do my very best for the road that we travel is long.
Now that the storm is over I can finally see the sun.
I can honestly claim a victory for this battle I have won.
I didn't win it alone for Jesus was always by my side.
When I thought that my strength was gone, He would take
me for a ride.
Blessed be the name of the Lord, for his mercy
endureth forever.
Even the storms belong to him for he made
all of the weather.
The Earth is the Lord's.

Blackman

Blackman Blackman you're being left behind.
If I didn't know any better I'd say that you're blind.
The decision is yours so what are you going to do?
Your destiny is in your own hands so it's left up to you.
Stop pointing your finger at everyone else.
You need to be honest and blame yourself.
You won't read you won't write you won't go to school.
You carry yourself like you are a fool.
The world is leaving you Blackman, Do you even care?
It's not in the shoes and the clothes that you wear.
Sean John, Hilfiger, Phat Farm, Roca wear.
Trying to be hip when nobody cares.
Walking around with your clothes hanging down.
Poor pitiful Blackman, you look like a clown.
If you would only devise a plan,
If you could have the whole world eating
out of your hand.
Life is too crucial this world plays for keeps.
Whatever you sow, that's what you reap.
No one cares for what you're going through.
They are constantly building new prisons just for you.

Blackman, Blackman you must understand that technology
is booming all across the land.
You need some training, get serious about school. With
60% failing, it's definitely not cool.
Poor lost Blackman what are you going to do?
The whole wide world is exterminating you.

Blackman, your mind is too terrible to waste!

Black Woman

Black woman, Black woman you're doing just fine.
Keep your head up and stay in line.
You're getting an education and moving up in the world.
You are indeed the original Black pearl.
Black woman, Black woman you are not alone.
Stay close to God, He will keep you strong.
Be aware of the thugs, He will bring you down. If you fall
in his trap you will be his clown.
Can't you see that they are preying on you to survive?
You are the one who is keeping them alive. You are the
ones who have a good job.
Thugs roam the streets looking for someone to rob.
God knows that it's hard working and going to school.
Yes knowledge and education is definitely a tool.
Jesus Christ is the only man that you need.
He will fill your void and feed your greed.
Don't allow a thug to dump their trash in you.
If you get pregnant then you'll be through.
They will load you down with a house full of kids.
Then find someone else to do their bid.
All men are not bad in fact some are good.
If you find one of those you need to knock on wood.

Black woman, Black woman keep doing what you do.
You don't need a man to validate you.
Please uphold yourself for a God sent man. Don't be in a
hurry, wait out God's plan.
You can be successfully happy, starting today.
But you can't let anything stand in your way.
Black woman, you owe it to yourself to be the best that
you can be.

Homeland

Everybody have a place that they call home.

In that place is where they belong.

That's the way that it supposes to be.

Everyone on this earth was born to be free.

The earth is a very massive place.

Inhabited with numerous different races.

Geographically situated on their own land.

Until everything got out of hand.

Greed came along and changed everything.

It also started the slavery ring.

Now black people's spirit will never be the same.

And we have no one but our ancestors to blame.

No one can come into your home,

To acquire something that they don't own.

So how can a few dominate the land?

They had help with their kidnapping plan.

For guns, clothe, knives and rum,

Kings sold flesh so slavery begun.

It continued to be a marketable trade.

That is the way the foundation was laid.

So as it grew, it got out of hand.

So millions of blacks were kidnapped from their land.

Voyage

Below the deck of the ship the conditions were bad.
Everywhere that you looked black faces was sad.
Every inch of the deck was covered with flesh.
They were lying in blood and all sort of mess.
Chained to a corpse here, giving birth over there.
The ones that were in charge didn't even care.
Very little to eat, very little to drink.
Urine and feces with unbearable stink.
Believe it or not it happened for real.
It was a miracle that anyone lived.
They all were insured so they expected some to die.
That's the reason that they piled them so high.
Sharks would always follow the boat.
They didn't give the dead bodies time to float.
The ones that survived wish that they had died.
For in the end they lost all their pride.
A deadly voyage it proved to be.
In America they would no longer be free.

Oppressed

How did it feel to be taken away?
And not get see your family another day.
Gagged and dragged all through the night.
Blindfolded just to hinder your sight.
What was it like to work all day?
Then get whipped because your cotton didn't weigh.
200 pounds are what you must pick or prepare to receive
the bull whip licks.
For physical punishment was always hard,
The skin from your back would easily part.
What was it like to be forbidden to read?
And used like an animal whose purpose is to breed.
What was it like to be raped and bear?
And violated until you are scared to sleep.
What was it like to have a tree on your back?
Then still have to drag that heavy cotton sack.
Should you stay, should you run away?
Will you hang from a tree one day?

The answers to these questions we will never know but
our ancestors had answers galore.
They endured to the end but it was hard.
But now they have no worries for they are in Heaven with
God.
They overcame . . .

Freeman

Now that I am told that I can go free.
I don't understand how that can be.
I don't understand what you expect me to do.
But I know that I can't stay here with you.
I don't have anywhere that I can go.
There is so much that I need to know.
I cannot write nor can I read.
What type of life am I to lead?
I have no money, I have no land.
I have no purpose, I have no plan.
But I won't let that bother me!
For I is a man and I is free.

I'm free at last, free at last, Thank God Almighty,
I'm free at last!

Amistad

Importing slave had been abolished all across the land.

The captain of the Amistad had devised a new plan.

They would guide their ship away from the shore.

Then head back to land to capture some more.

They were being very careful to stay out of sight.

So they were forced to do all of their business at night.

Their plan was only to capture the strong, get a ship full
and head back home.

Every victim that they captured was stored in a jail, with
no idea that they would soon set sail.

They were made to exercise to keep them strong, for the
voyage to America would be very long.

No sooner than they had gotten a full load, they were
cuffed and shackled and herded on board.

No doubt they were headed for the slavery ring; some of
them had dignity of that of a king.

Because their captors wouldn't settle for less. They had no
idea that they had captured the best.

There were might warriors who were willing to
fight to the end.

No matter what happened they fought to win.

They were never satisfied being treated that way.

So they always kept looking for that special day.
A day when their captors would mistakenly slip, to get an opportunity to take over the ship.
Finally an opportunity came their way; they searched for their captors to make the pay.
Some were killed and some rowed out to sea, everything had changed so quickly.
They spared the captains to take them back home.
They had no idea that they were being steered wrong.
For they were traveling by sight and didn't have a map.
Deceived and led right into a trap.
They landed in America and were put in jail.
After a long court battle justice prevailed.
They were eventually set free and allowed to go home.
Back to the place where they belong.

Harriett Tubman

The black Moses was the greatest woman of all time.
She helped more slaves to escape than everyone
else combined.
Even while she was alive she made history, exactly when
she was born is a mystery.
It was believed to be around 1820, there were no records
for they didn't keep any.
Her parent were brought to America in chains,
From a West African tribe with the Ashantis name.
Their slave name was Benjamin Ross and Harriett Green.
They had 11 children to add to the slavery ring.
Harriett was rented out at 5 years old; she slept on the
kitchen floor even in the cold.
She wore a tag like cows and shared scraps with the dogs.
She ran away as a child and slept with the hogs.
She refused to help her master by holding a run away,
He did something to make her remember that day.
She was hit in the head by a 2lb weight, that why she
would remember that date.
She was unconscious and in a coma for a full 2 weeks,
while here master brought in buyers by the fleet.

She never got accustomed to doing housework, she
enjoyed outside playing in dirt.
She was a very good worker in fact one of the best her
strength could put any man to the test.
She always dreamed of the Mason Dixie line, she had no
idea it was a sign.
She married John Tubman in 1844, He was dear to her and
she loved him so.
After 5 years of marriage she was force to go, did she kiss
John goodbye nobody know.
She came back to save her family and friends, the
Underground Railroad was definitely a win.
He had people in high places that had safe houses
and supplies.
She was also a master of disguise.
She drugged babies with opium to keep them from crying.
Her favorite song was Moses go down.
She never lost one slave and I'll tell you why, because her
motto was "Move or Die"

The Blacks History

As we celebrate Black History, I can only tell you what
it means to me. I can only you how I feel, a lot of Blacks
have died so that we might live. We are all different in
our own special way, some of you maybe famous one day,
some prominent Blacks have paved the way so listen to
these words that I am about to say.
Harriett Tubman couldn't read or write but she helped 300
slaves escape through the night.
They called her the Black Moses, a master of disguise; they
offered $40,000 as a reward prize.
Frederick Douglass was a great educator, A Marshall, A
recorder, a journalist and Orator.
Rosa Parks was on her way home, at the back of the bus
she didn't belong.
She was arrested and put in jail which started a boycott that
went very well.
George Washington Carver was one of a kind; He was the
greatest agriculture scientist of all time.
Madam C. J. Walker with her formula to straighten, hair
was the first Black woman to become a millionaire.
Louis Armstrong could not be stopped, bought his first
horn at the pawnshop.

Duke Ellington wrote over 2000 songs, In France the highest honors he won.

Dr. Charles R. Drew founded the first blood bank. So he's still saving lives that what AI think.

Thomas A. Dorsey with the first gospel band sang precious Lord please take my hand.

Langston Hughes was a very gifted man; the poems that he wrote will always stand.

Nat King Cole with his TV show was a pianist and the 1st black host that we know.

The first black female surgeon was Dr. Dorothy Brown; Irvin C. Mollison was the first black judge around.

The first black general was Daniel James; Alex Haley was crown with the Pulitzer fame.

Marcus Garvey was a very powerful man; it was by him that civil rights began.

Malcolm X was a many of many words, all over the world his voice was heard.

Maya Angelo knows why the caged bird sings and Dr. Martin Luther King made freedom ring.

So now it's your time, what are you going to do? History still holds a place for you.

Garrett A. Morgan

So many blacks have paved the way.
Some of the things that they did saved us today.
A lot of the things that they invented are mysteries untold.
But unto our society, they're more precious than gold.
Let's step back in time when the world was new.
To ask an inventor what would we do?
Garrett A. Morgan, if it wasn't for you,
inventing your gas mask,
What would we do?
They didn't want your idea, they thought it was jive.
Until a bomb ripped through tunnel number 5.
Deadly gases, smoke and dust filled the underground space.
Then they remembered that your mask won first place.
They contacted you in a hurry and asked you to come.
You brought your gas mask and got the job done.
You and your brother were named heroes of the day.
You led the rescue team by showing them the way.
At the end of the day, 32 people were saved.
And your mask started selling in a mighty wave.
When they found out that the inventor was black.

Some orders were cancelled and some were sent back.
But no matter what happened you didn't give in
You knew in your heart that one day you would win.
Then you started a company as a businessman.
Then invented the traffic light, now it's all over the land.

Howard University

Howard University is a school of our own.
It's truly a place that we can call home.
1876 is when it was found.
1877 they completed the ground.
General Oliver O. Howard is where it got its name.
He was the founder and head of the
Freedman Bureau acclaim.
Established by the war department in 1865.
As an act of Congress to help Black people strive.
It furnished food, wages and medical supplies.
Working conditions, schools and distributed land
was supervised.
Howard College of medicine opened in 1868.
The civil war had ended 3 years to that date.
Because of society's segregation rules, most blacks couldn't
go to the white medical schools.
Howard has trained a large percentage of blacks.
To be competent doctors and on the right track.
Today Howard University is still training the best.
Just ask Bill Cosby, He wouldn't settle for less.
So if you want to be a doctor and don't know where to go.
Just find your way to Howard and open the door.

You hold the key to your own success.

Thank You Dr. King

We truly thank you Dr. Martin Luther King.
Where would we be if you didn't have your dream?
Where would we be if you weren't so brave?
Would we be free or would we still be enslaved.
We thank you Dr. King for everything that
you went through.
We know that it took a lot of courage too.
We thank you Dr. King for being a great man.
For boycotting and marching all over the land.
We thank you Dr. King for every night you spent in jail.
Even if you were afraid no one could even tell.
Rosa Parks thank you for standing up for her.
It helped to change the buses from the way that they were.
When God created you, He made a mighty man.
Your voice was heard all over the land.
Coretta was blessed to have you by her side.
She was right there with you on every freedom ride.
I know that she thanked you for the children that
you helped her bore.
One of them maybe the essence of your core.

So we give thanks to you Dr. King, a great and
wonderful man.
And we will try to live our lives according to your plan.

Dr. Martin Luther King Jr., we thank God for you and
your dream . . .

Coretta

There was no greater woman than Mrs. Coretta
Scott-King.
Without a doubt in our eyes you will always be a queen.
In front of every great woman there is a great man.
Your husband will always be famous all across the land.
He would have never succeeded without you by his side.
You and all of your children were Dr. King's
ultimate pride.
You gave up your career just to help him along the way.
With your strength you kept him strong after a long
troubled day.
Dr. King was truly blessed to have you on his side.
No one knows how you felt the day that
your husband died.
He went to the mountaintop and saw the Promised Land.
So you don't have to worry for He's in our Father's hand.
He has saved a place for you for he loves
you with all of his heart.
When the 2 of you meet in Heaven I know that you'll
never depart.

Many women have done virtuous things but you have
exceeded them all.
You always kept your dignity and you taught
women not to fall.

The world thank you for being who you were.

We honor You

The American pride

You can't hide the American Pride.
Its distinctive characteristics shines from inside.
It's truly a wonderful possession for us all to behold.
It's inside of all the youth as well as the old.
It's a feeling that locked deep within that is
impossible to explain.
Once a foreigner turns American they will
never be the same.
It doesn't matter where in America you may choose to be.
Once you are on American soil you are indeed free.
Free to live your life and free to be yourself.
Living in peace and harmony along beside everyone else.
You have a freedom of choice and a freedom of speech.
And your goal can be whatever you choose to reach.
Many have been born and many have died.
But no one can ever extinguish The American pride.

Aren't you proud to be an American?

Katrina

Almighty Awesome Katrina is what the world called me.
I was the biggest and worst Hurricane
that you ever did see.
I'm an instrument of God and as deadly as could be.
Nothing in this world can stand up to me.
I started in the ocean as a tropical depression. I picked up
my motion and started a recession.
I crept upon the coast stalking out my prey. My ultimate
intention was to spoil everyone's day.
I swooped upon the land at 175 miles per hour.
I put fear in the hearts of man with my
awesome super power.
I caused the worst and greatest disaster that
this world has ever seen.
I distressed Biloxi Mississippi and destroyed New Orleans.
I evacuated the entire city leaving people nowhere to go.
The where-a-bout of some love ones,
some people still don't know.
I put chaos and confusion at an all time high.
Some people were unfortunate, I'm sorry they had to die.
I destroyed everything that was positioned that was
positioned in my path.

I know that you all was wondering just
how long I would last.
Houses, buildings, cars, trees were no match for me. I tore
down the levee and made room for the sea.
Then we flooded the entire land and
invaded all the homes.
Now complete cities are scattered in places
where they don't belong.
I've already cost Americans a trillion dollars or more.
I am unlike anything that you
have ever experienced before.
It's true that I was on a mission for our Almighty God,
And you can bet your bottom dollar that
I sincerely did my job.
I am sorry for all the pain and trouble that I caused. You
have my sympathy for the love ones that you lost.
You should learn a lesson from me and do what
God want you to do.
So please don't blame me for he sent me to you.
For God is the Supreme Being, residing in the infinite sky.
I am at his disposal and will always be standing by.
To the world, "You better change and
don't forget my name."
Now I can rest in peace in the Hurricane Hall of Fame!
Oh what an awesome God we serve . . .

Mighty Katrina

All that I have I give unto you Only God knows
what you are to do.
Only God can help you to win this fight.
Some or your lives will never be right.
We all know what happened and how it began.
But is this the beginning or is it the end.
We must be strong for this is our test.
The strong will survive but I pity the rest.
We were separated, alienated, pitched and tossed. Some of
which in we love are forever lost.
It doesn't get any worse than what happened on that day.
God let Might Katrina have her way.
We can't blame Katrina for she was only doing her job.
Her mission was to evaluate, annihilate and rob.
Katrina had no mercy, she brought only pain. Destroying
the land while claiming her fame.
Why did God allow it? We can all ask why.
But our answer only lies with God up high.
We must be very careful of how we choose to live.
Sometimes we deserve the things that God gives.
God has destroyed the whole world before; we are all
standing at the last door.

God will not put on us more that we can bear.
When it gets too hard, he will always be right there.
So stand strong in your faith and try not to fall.
Build on your future so you can stand tall.
Your life may get better than it was before. You hold the
key to open that door.
Don't accept the rumors that this is the end.
Just put your trust in Jesus and start all over again.
You can make it . . .

Misery

I have only bad memories of what happen
on that dreadful day.
It seems like the end of the world and everything was being
blown away.
It seem like the whole world was coming to an end.
I didn't see any way that we could possibly win.
We were in a fight against the mighty fury of God.
I've never seen his mighty winds ever blow so hard.
I've never seen such cruel darkness engulfing the sky.
I'd never seen the flood waters rise so very high.
Katrina was playing no games; in fact she was
playing for keeps.
Leaving lost souls for the grim Reaper to reap.
What did we do to deserve this? For God to let
her have her way!
We were all speechless with absolutely no words to say.
We were all terrorized with no earthly place to go.
The winds were so devastating with its might horrifying
blow.
There was noting that we could do and nowhere that we
could hide.

Our entire city was engulfed and Katrina was taking
us for a ride.
We could only hold on and hope for the best.
For The Mighty Katrina's fury was nothing like the rest.
But in the mist of all the madness I could still feel
God's hand.
He was calming the storm and reclaiming all the land.
Indeed he has destroyed the entire land before.
The reason why he does these things, we may never know.
But in the midst of everything God still has his way.
Even the storms and the elements of the earth obey
whatever he says.
So I thank you God for it all the good as well as the bad.
And ask you to lift my spirit and don't let me be so sad.
That I lost some one that I love . . . .
God Bless us all . . .

Spared

August 30, 2005 is the day that Katrina came alive.
She was wandering around all over the place.
Then she hit the town with finesse and grace.
There was nowhere to run and nowhere to hide.
She was everywhere and dominating outside.
She was snatching up trees and turning over cars.
Destroying homes and wiping out bars.
I was so amazed that I couldn't believe my eyes.
I had to snap out of a daze just to save some lives.
I started with my own for I was in a bind.
Katrina had trapped me and I was dying.
I can't let this happen, this just can't be.
Death is all around roaming ever so free.
My family needs me so I can't give in.
I have to fight, Katrina can't win.
Just when it seem like it was over and done.
God gently steeped in and the battle was won.
He seized Katrina and sent her away.
Once again God saved the day.
For the mighty Katrina was too awesome to bear.
God showed me again just how much he care.

By keeping me alive . . .

Banished

To all who are in exile this poem is just for you.
It maybe a guide to tell you what to do.
It may include instructions to which you should heed.
Just submit to its message and follow its lead.
Perhaps you did nothing to deserve life being this way.
Katrina left us all with no words to say.
You may be in a situation where you don't
know what to do.
Heed to this message for God is speaking to you.
It's his will than one day we will all die.
We have a home for us in his infinite sky.
We all have a place where we will go.
It's all in God's hand so we'll never know.
You may be worried, you may be sad! You may be
confused, you may be mad!
What else can you do here in your time of despair?
When you are in exile it seems like nobody care.
The life that you have known is so far away. Now you've
found yourself living from day to day.
You may be separated from the ones that you love.
The only place that you can turn to is God above.
Your fellow Americans are doing all that they can do.

But God is the only one who can pull you through.

He loves you dearly, you are his child. He can send you back home in style.

God can make your life better than it was before. Jesus is knocking just open the door.

Open the door to your heart and let him in. You got to trust him if you want to win.

Nobody knows the things that you do; they are open to God but secrets to you.

But you don't have to worry and you don't have to cry.

Jesus is waiting for you so just give him a try.

He'll make a way out of no way . . . .

Home

There is no place like home!
There is no place like home!
It's true, there is no place like home . . .
In life and living it's the only place you belong.
That's the only place that makes you feel good.
It is your comfort zone and has all that it should.
It has everything that you like and everything
that you need.
It is a place that you can prepare, to succeed.
It maybe a shack nestled in the valley below.
Or it may be a mansion on a hill that you love to show.
It maybe something that no one wants to own.
But to you it's your castle that you call home.
Your home maybe different from all the homes
that you know.
But your home is your refuge and you love it so.
Even though it seems like everything has gone wrong.
Just put your faith and trust in Jesus and he will
take you back home.

Jesus is the way the truth and the light.
He will guide your way through the day and the night.

There is no place like home.
If you trust him he will take you back home.

I Am

I am the Almighty and will always be.

Everything that exists was made by me.

I can do anything that my heart desire.

I made heave above and Hell equipped with fire.

I made the Earth, The Universe and everything within.

I refuse to tolerate wickedness, abomination and sin.

I made all of the oceans, the rivers and the seas.

I made all of the creatures, the birds and the bees.

I made all of the weathers, the sun and the rain.

I made all of the storms, tornados and hurricanes.

I also made you just to have and behold.

There are so many things that I made that the mystery
wont unfold.

I can do any and everything that I may choose to do.

And you are not to question me for I don't answer to you.

What you really need to do is get your life right.

For my only begotten son Jesus will soon be coming back.

I am willing to make your life better that it was before.

For you are my pride and joy and I really love you so.

I AM that I AM

Study to show yourself approved and accepted before God.

God

God you are the only one who knows what's happening or
how things should go.
Your ways are not like our ways so that means that we will
never know.
No matter what happens it is only by your hands.
Sometimes we allow Satan to carry out his wicked plans.
Even then you're in control and always have your way.
You make mysteries to unfold each and every day.
You sit high on your throne a holy place indeed.
Then you watch us do our wrong just like an evil seed.
You hope that we choose what's right for you
let us have our way.
But why do you let us fight and spoil each other's day.
War is dreadfully wrong for innocent people will die.
And all of the times that we are fighting we don't know
the reason why.
We should never get discouraged when thing
get really hard.
When the only thing that we must do is to look to you
Our God.

Dear God just keep showing us the way . . .

Look out

I was observing the twin towers dominating the sky.
When I noticed a 747 plane soaring up very high.
All of a sudden it dipped, and started to fly too low.
I thought that it didn't know which way that it was
supposed to go.
As I continued to observe it started to come near.
I noticed that the buildings were much too tall for the
plane to clear.
I thought that the pilot had made a serious mistake.
I noticed that the plane was going much too fast and it had
gotten too late.
Too late to rise and too late to turn.
It hit tower # 1 and started to burn.
It hit so hard and it happened so fast.
It damaged the foundation, so the building couldn't last.
As Tower #1 started to fall, Tower #2 remained
standing tall.
Then right before my eyes, another plane appeared
to my surprise.
It proceeded to hit tower # 2.
In a matter of minutes both towers were through.
They burst into flames and tumbled to the ground.

Thus leaving dead bodies scattered all around.

We will never forget that dreadful day.

This took a lot of our love ones away.

It definitely was a merciless act indeed.

We still don't know where this will lead.

The only thing that we can do is put it in God's hand.

For he is the only one that can save our land.

911

September 11, 2001 is the day that it all begun.
Before we could arise out of our bed.
The attack was coming straight ahead.
To them we didn't do anything.
So why would they want to hijack our plane?
They used it like it was a bomb.
They hit our buildings and caused great harm.
Now over a thousand of our people are dead.
And we may be going to war instead.
War is bad because a lot of people will die.
We don't know where and we don't know how.
God please help us because war is no fun.
To you can we dial 911?
God please Bless the world . . .

American

United we stand and divided we fall.
We have no one else to call.
We have a big problem but we are not alone.
We are capable of taking care of our own.
It all started on a Tuesday morning
It was a surprise we had no warning.
We showed them love and taught them to fly.
We had no clue that they wanted us to die.
Our very own plans were used against us.
Now we are wondering who we can trust.
What can we say? What can we do?
Someone is at fault and we think that we know who.
Should a whole nation suffer because of one man?
Would it be right to destroy their land?
Let us all look to God for He knows what is best.
We are being put through the ultimate test.
It hurts us deadly for countless lives were lost.
And to rebuild our nation would definitely cost.
We will recover but it will take time.

Let's stop being so trusting and being so kind.
Home of the brave and land o the free.
There is no place that I'd rather be . . .
Than in America . . .
I am proud to be an American

Wanted

Osama Bin Laden, we wanted you dead or alive.
There was nowhere to run and nowhere to hide.
Everywhere you went you leave people dead.
We had a price on your head.
You had nowhere to run and you had nothing to do?
It was only a matter of time but now we got you.
You should have died by your hands and killed yourself.
So we didn't have to kill no one else.
We almost destroyed a nation because of you.
You should have had compassion for your people
Because we told you that you were through.

Doomed

We are trapped in this building just waiting here to die.
The terrorist brought death to us from our planes in the
sky.
People are falling all around me there is panic everywhere.
There is too much smoke to see and the pain is hard to
bear.
Some glass has hit me; I can feel some cuts in my face.
I got to keep moving but I'm caught in a maze.
God please help me, I'm trapped on 50th floor.
It would certainly be a blessing if I could get to the
Door.
I hope that I'm not doomed and this is not my time to
Die.
I didn't even get the chance to tell my family bye.

Fear

A catastrophe has happen and I am very scared.
All that I have left is the memories that we shared.
What will happen to my kids?
What will happen to my wife?
What will happen to me? Will I lose my life?
I never thought that this could happen.
This can't be for real.
I hope that this isn't the last day that I will get to live.
I have never felt fear like I feel today.
The only thing that I could do is kneel down and pray.

Angels Around

There are angels all around us, saving people
everywhere.
Wrapping their wings around us, administering love
and care.
They were dispatched by God to help us to be safe.
Satan presence is here along with ferocious blaze.
He's here to steal souls to take them down to hell.
That is the only place that he wants us to dwell.
We are blessed to have God's angels, saving us one by
one.
And they will never stop until their job is done.

Where

Where are you my friend?
I can't see you anywhere.
I can't leave you here because for you I really care.
But what am I suppose to do surrounded by all of this fire?
Wives are seeking their husbands and husbands are
seeking their Wives.
For they are missing parts of each other's lives.
Up under tons of rubble, countless lives are lost.
The whole idea is senseless for it happened without a
Cause.
God please help us, this pain is hard to bear.
No matter where this takes us, we know that you'll be
there.

Save Me

Which way do I run?
I don't know which away to go.
As soon as it began, the ceiling hit the floor.
I see my best friend lying in a fresh pool of blood.
Now a wave of innocent people is coming in a flood.
Let us all help each other, for it is the only way.
Or none of us will live to see another day.
Before we start our journey, let's all join hand in hand.
And give our praises to God before we take a stand.
I'll help save you, if you help save me.
God will save us both and help us to be free.

The Heroes

Polices and Firefighters were everywhere.
People dead and alive were scattered here and there.
The fearless Firefighters were going in and out.
Their jobs were dangerous for the fire was hot.
Polices were controlling and keeping people in line.
Dust was everywhere so they had to lead the blind.
Doctors and nurses were working as a team.
They saw things that they had never seen.
Everything that they all had to learn was put to the test.
They were all heroes; some were husbands and some
were wives.
Some were husbands and some were wives.
But they all were brave and had a job to do.
They saved so many, did they save you?
You all are true American and we give thanks to God.
And we'll forever be thanking you from the bottom of
our Heart.

Crash

If the stock market crash, what will it do?
How will it affect me and you?
What will happen if everyone lost their job?
Will that make an honest man rob?
No matter what, happens life must go on.
Everyone needs a place to call home.
What if we can't afford to live?
What if the government has nothing to give?
There are millions of questions when you're short on cash
Times are very hard when the economy crash.
Keep giving Glory to God for he's still live large.
Just be faithful to Him and keep moving on.
Keep in mind that this Earth is not our home.

Maintain

Our economy is in trouble.
There are layoffs every day.
The tragedy of 911 has gotten it this way.
Jobs that were once secured, that we thought were here to
Stay.
Now that this has happen, are vanishing and going away.
The economy is a system that we all have to share.
But what can we do at a time like this when there are
Layoffs everywhere.
We must continue to live because life will go on.
This is no time to be a weakling; to survive you must be
Strong.
So get your head together, and put your feet on solid
Ground.
Then do your very best to let nothing get you down.

Gone

Today I came to work with a smile upon my face.
I had the slightest idea that it would soon erase.
As I clocked in and proceeded to go to work.
I noticed that all of my co-workers were
looking kind of hurt.
When I asked them what was wrong,
they only shook their head.
I found out that my job was gone;
I thought that I'd drop dead.
I couldn't believe my ears; I thought that it was a dream.
I've been working here for years, my job means everything.
What will I do now? Time has gotten so hard.
The one thing that I will do is keep my faith in God.

My Job

My job was special with very decent pay.

By having a job like mine, I lived a special way.

Along with my pay, my family was insured.

My job made me felt very secured.

I often went to work five days a week.

With every night and weekend off which made it easy to

Sleep.

With my job, I could afford everything that I needed.

Now that it is gone, I don't know where this will lead.

Will I lose my house?

Will I lose my car?

Will I lose my life if I go to war?

No one knows what the future may hold.

Just trust God and watch your riches unfold.

Help

Looking for help? Where will I go?
You can't go begging at the grocery store.
You can't go begging at the car lot.
They are only interested in what you got.
If you don't have no money and you don't have a job.
And you refuse to steal and you refuse to rob.
Where do you go when you need a little help?
It's just like a baby trying to take its first step.
The chances are that you certainly will fall.
It may be better to stay on knees and crawl.
While you're crawling, look the right way.
Then God will help you to walk again one day.
Prosperity is coming, trouble don't last.
All of this present will soon past.

Survival

Surviving the game, Life is a test.

In order to be superior, you have to beat the best.

There situations and circumstances that we face

every day.

We must endure for we can't run away.

You mustn't give up no matter what goes wrong.

Sometimes you may find yourself standing all alone.

Me, I'm a survival; I'll never give in.

There is desire burning inside of me that is pushing me to

Win.

Even though I'm trying to win there is a chance that I may

Fall.

But I'll still keep moving forward even if I have to crawl.

Winners never quit and quitters never win.

In order to be a survival you must endure to the end.

Men of Honor

I'm going into this building to save all the lives that I can.
There is a chance that I may not survive
but this is my plan!
Firefighting is a job that I have pledged to do. I will never
story trying until I'm through.
I will never give up no matter what goes wrong. And I will
keep singing this same old song.
I am a fearless Firefighter who is saving all the
lives that I can.
I have had people lives expire right in my hand. I have had
to save the young as well as the old.
To go in a burning building you have to be bold.
September 11, 2001 was a day that held no fun.
During some merciful attacks many people were killed. It
was certainly a test of skills
There was very little that we could do,
When we go to the sight the building was through.
There were tons of rubble piled everywhere. Bodies and
parts were scattered here and there.
We did everything that we could do;
we lost a lot of brave men too!

Approximately 300 firefighters lost their lives. This left a lot
of grieving husbands and wives.
For every life lost, two was saved. At the end of the day,
The Banner yet waved.
We regret what happen but we will do it all again!
For we are the men of Honor and this is our Plan.

<u>"I am Proud to be a Firefighter"</u>

Your Hero

You lost your Hero and I know that you're sad. It is only
human for you to be mad.
I know that you were devastated and confused.
When you heard the tragedy all over the news.
A tragedy like that was hard to believe. Losing your love
one was hard to conceive.
Now you are still wondering what you can do.
Your Hero's strength always pulls you through. Your hero
is still right by your side.
You should b e honored for they died with pride.
Nobody knows how you feel; you are still wondering
is this for real.
You had to accept it but it was hard, you had to
keep looking to God.
It's not easy to let go because you love him so much.
You will always be longing just to feel his touch.
All Firefighter are heroes for they are a special breed. They
are the people that this world need.
Without our Firefighters what will we do? We need them
here to pull us through.
They are trained to be here whenever we call.
I feel that they are the bravest people of all.

They put their lives on the line every.
And they definitely don't do it for their meager pay.
They do it because they are one of a kind. Heroes like
yours are hard to find.
So you don't have to worry and you don't have to cry.
Your hero has his honor and wings in the infinite sky.

Your Hero is an Angel who is always by your side . . .

My Hero

I lost my Hero and my am I sad. It is only human for me to be mad.

I know that you were devastated and confused.

When I heard the tragedy all over the news.

A tragedy like that was hard to believe. Losing my love one was hard to conceive.

Now I am still wondering what I can do.

My Hero's strength always pulls me through. My hero is still right by my side.

I am truly honored for he died with pride.

Nobody knows how I feel; I am still wondering is this for real.

I had to accept it but it was hard, I had to keep looking to God.

It's not easy to let go because you love him so much.

I will always be longing just to feel his touch.

All Firefighter are heroes for they are a special breed. They are the people that this world need.

Without our Firefighters what will we do? We need them here to pull us through.

They are trained to be here whenever we call. I feel that they are the bravest people of all.

They put their lives on the line every. And they definitely
don't do it for their meager pay.
They do it because they are one of a kind. Heroes like
yours are hard to find.
So I don't have to worry and I don't have to cry.
My hero has his honor and wings in the infinite sky.

My Hero is an Angel who is always by your side . . .

Golden memories

To lose a love on is always hard.

It makes us want to question God.

It makes us want to ask him why.

The one that we love was called up high.

There is a mystery in death that no one knows.

But it's certain that one day that we all must go.

God has a place for us all.

We have no choice but to answer his call.

Remember the good times that you always shared.

And think about how much you all really cared.

Clifford life on earth was not in vain.

Unto society he was a gain.

The wife that he had and the children that he bore.

Will always love him perhaps even more.

More than anyone may ever know.

Within their actions it will always show.

Within their hearts it will certainly behold.

Those golden sweet memories that are solid gold.

Lord help us to be strong and accept your will.

For it's by your grace that we all can live.

Help us to be stronger with each passing day.

Comfort us entirely and wipe our tears away.

Raw Deal

It is totally unfair as to how the world treat people today.
A human life is not something that we should throw away.
A human life is precious for it is a gift from God.
It may be easy or it can be hard.
When two people get married their life is joined.
The two lives are supposed to live as one.
For better or for worst until death do them apart.
Those vows are sacred unto almighty God.
Terry Shervious's husband should be ashamed.
He treated her like it was a game.
Living with and loving another woman while insisting that
she die.
Is truly a raw deal and we are all asking why.
Why was he allowed to treat her that way?
Her dedicated parents could not have her say.
If he didn't want her he should have given her back.
Allowing her to suffer was cruel and not right.
It was a test from God to judge her fate.
He failed the test and now it's too late.

But her family doesn't have to worry and
they don't have to cry.
For God is nourishing Terry in the infinite sky.

Let not all men be judged by the evil deeds of Mr.
Shervios.

Remember

De'Shonda I know that it's hard for you to go on.
For the love of me and my daughter
I need you to be strong.
I need you to be strong in each and every way.
I will be beside you each and every day.
I will always b e beside you no matter
what you go through.
I don't have to say that I am still in love with you.
I don't have to tell you how happy you made me.
It was because of you that I was the best that I could be.
No one will ever know just how much that I did for you.
I know that you won't ever forget that
my love for you is true.
I may not be able to ever touch you again, but I can still
see your face.
I know that no other man will ever take my place.
Always show me that smile that I love to see.
I will never forget you so don't forget me.
I want you to remember the good times that outweigh
the bad.

Close your eyes visualize my face whenever you are sad.
Learn to be happy although it will never be the same.
We must accept God's will for there is nothing that we
can change.
Don't ever blame God and do continue to pray.
That he will unite our marriage in his
glorious heaven one day.

De'shonda carry on for me it's your time to shine.

True Champion

Albert James Lucas this tribute is just for you.
You have touched a lot of lives and you changed some too.
You will forever be remembered at Northeast the school
that you served with pride.
You have always been a role model and
we are forever on your side.
You were granted a full athletic scholarship
for the things that you did.
Troy State University was fortunate for they won your bid.
They were very lucky for not being far from home.
This made it easy for your family to follow you along.
De Shonda was your pride, Mariah was your joy.
Leonard was the one that taught you as a boy.
David and Elaine were there to provide all of your needs.
They are the ones that planted all those seeds.
Towering 6 feet tall in stature and weighing 300 pounds.
Everyone sorted you advice whenever you came around.
You were an all American champion exploiting
examples for us to see.
You always tried to be the best that you could be.

A lineman in the field and a teacher in the classroom.

A well rounded gentleman playing to any tune.

We will all miss you but we will keep you in our heart.

For everyone that you helped could give thanks to God.

Anyone that ever met you could very proudly say:

"I once met a champion; He smiled and looked my way".

"Be strong and play on is what Big Luke would say:

To the team of Los Angeles Avengers,

"For me go all the way".

Seventy-Six

David and Elaine Lucas and family our
prayers go out to you.
No words could ever explain what you are going through.
We all understand and we do feel your pain.
Your son is a great lost and your lives won't be the same.
Al was a great person and he represented us all.
We are all so proud of him for succeeding in pro football.
You reared a great child that will go down in history.
This kind of thing seldom occurs and is still a mystery.
A will be missed by people great and small.
But he will be missed by the family most of all.
Very few people could make it as a pro.
You gave Al the courage to succeed where ever he may go.
Perhaps you taught your son that there was
nothing that he couldn't do.
His freedom of choice, success and inspiration
all reflect upon you.
To join the family business representing people
all over the land.
Were possibly his intentions in his life goal plans.

You allowed him to do some of the things that
he really wanted to do.
He only wanted to stand alone and be a
blessing to both of you.
He was still in the family business for he represented us all.
He wore jersey # 76 standing proud and tall.
To you David and Elaine, we know that you did your best.
For your son Al made it and he never settled for less.
So you don't have to worry and you don't have to cry.
#76 is now with God and playing in the infinite sky.

Perhaps

Mildred was my wife, perhaps you all know.
I wonder if you knew her, if in fact it could be so.
I wonder if you knew the way that she use to told.
Or maybe you remember the way that she use to walk.
Did you ever know that she really loved the Lord?
I know that she gave Jesus her whole humble heart.
I know for myself that she was as wonderful
as she could be.
She was my wife and she showed that side to me.
I know that she might have shown a lot of love to you.
If she did then you already know that
what I am saying is true.
She gave me tow beautiful children and
left them for me to love.
We use to all fit together like a hand inside of a glove.
Now she has gone to God and left this cold, cruel world.
She had time to clean her heart and manifest into a pearl.
Blessed are the ones that suffer for
it puts them close to God.
They have nothing else to do but give Jesus their heart.
For sudden death is present and will gladly take you there.

You may not even get a warning and
may leave without a prayer.
So we don't have to cry for Mildred knew
which way to go.
The spirit of God taught me so I could let her know.
Perhaps Mildred got her wings . . .

A Great Man

We lost a great man in Senator Robert Brown.
I don't know if he had one enemy in this whole town!
He had been in politics for 20 long years.
In the House of Senate he had so much to give.
He was a man of integrity and a man of explicit pride.
The whole State of Georgia lost for
he was always on our side.
He had always fought our battles and he never gave up.
He did not tolerate a government that was openly corrupt.
He was always honest and fair in each and every way. He
was a man of his word and did just what he says.
He knew how to change Macon,
but we didn't give him a shot.
He wanted to clean up our streets for our
blocks are always hot.
Our beautiful city is diminishing and
we have lost a great man.
I was blessed to be his friend for he told me his master plan.
I am lost for words and don't know what to say.
My good friend Robert Brown decided to go away.

We don't know what happened or
what he was going through.
All I know is that I had a friend that really loved me too.
I met a million people but none with greater pride.
But Senator Robert Brown always stood out in a crowd.
Robert Brown is gone but he will never be forgotten . . .

A Better Macon

Macon needs a Mayor like Senator Robert Brown.
He is the best candidate in the whole town!
He has been in politics for 20 long years.
In the House of Senate he had so much to give.
He is a man of integrity and a man of pride.
We need him as Mayor of Macon forever on our side.
He will fight all of our battles thus never giving up.
He will not tolerate a government that is corrupt.
He is honest and fair in each and every way.
He is a man of his word and does what he says.
He knows just what to do, so let's give him a shot.
He will clean up our streets for our blocks are hot.
Our beautiful city is diminishing but it needs to expand.
We need the right Mayor with a master plan.
Want a better Macon?
Elect a better Mayor!
Robert Brown is the Best Mayor for a Better Macon!

Brother T-Bo Greene

My brother was a man that stood on his own. In each and
every way he showed that he was strong.
Brother always did what he had to do and would do
anything to help me or you.
He didn't have very much education butt With God he
definitely had a good relation.
He loved the Bible, "that was a book he could read"! It's
like God taught him how thus planting the seed.
He was a collector of goods that people threw away. Those
things were valuable and He got paid every day.
He always saw good in everything. Now my Brother has
gone to receive his wings.
To his wonderful wife Mary whom he loved so much, I
know that you will forever miss his touch.
I know that you will keep Brother in your heart and the
two of you will never be apart.
To his daughter, Rolena, Mary and Annette,
your daddy was a man.
You all at times had him eating out of your hand.
To his sons Marshall and Bo-Pete. He gave you values and
taught you to be meek.

To your sister Sarah yall had a special bond; the way you
two interacted was so much fun.
To Cherie and Renee, He raised both of you so I know
that he loved yall too.
To me He was Brother, we shared the same mother and I
know that there will never be another.
We loved our Mother so very much it's like we both gave
each other her own special touch.
We saw our Mother when we looked in each other eyes
and it made us both realize.
That we had a bond that would never end that would
survive the trials through thick and thin.
You may meet our Mother on her Birthday please tell her
to continue to shine my way.
Tell Mama and Daddy that I still love them so and there is
one thing that I want you to know.
Having a brother like you gave me a reason to live and I
always had so much love to give, to you
I will cherish the time that we spent together . . .
Your Sister Kate

The Man

Look at me, I am a star.

I started from the bottom, but I've came far.

Far from what I use to be.

My own determination has set me free.

I reached for the moon but it was too far.

In my pursuit I captured a star.

I became who I am I found my way.

I assumed my identity and conquered the day.

Today is tomorrow for the life that we lead.

It will bring you much sorrow if your goals

are not achieved.

It is not a shame not to conquer your goal.

But it is a pity to have no dreams to behold.

I thank God everyday for helping me to win.

Before he came I didn't know where to begin.

Me I'm just Chauncey.

One man in this land

.I found my identity.

God gave me a plan.

I am being the best that I can be

Time

To watch the sun set and see the moon rise is a
heavenly sight unto our eyes.
To walk upon a sandy beach and have the
ocean within your reach.
To sit upon the mountain side and
watch the birds fly into the clouds.
To travel around or sail the sea,
these are the things that makes us free.
Contrary to what we all have heard,
captivity is not even for the birds.
A caged bird will sing to be set free while
beating the bars repeatedly.
Captivity encompasses freedom and dilapidates ones pride.
It diminishes the light that once shined inside.
Time is of essence it comes and goes,
it's full of happiness, joy and woes.
Incarceration is cruel with time as a debt,
time to deteriorate, time to regret.
If you did the crime you should do the time,
but not make examples for justice is blind.

Freedom is the most valuable commodity
that God gave to man.
We can't let the judicial system change God's Plan
Mistakes are made by us all every day, but it should not
take 30 years in prison to repay.
For the mistake that Marshall Greene made.

Join the Free Marshall Movement Today

Home

Covington Church is the place to be.

Visit our home site and you will see.

Our church family is so full of love.

It had to be appointed from God above.

The spirit of the Lord dwells within us.

God gave us a preacher that we can trust.

A preacher is a teacher doing the will of God.

Bringing forth the light which diminishes the dark.

There is an abundance of talent all over the place.

Including Pamela the artist producing music with grace.

The dedication of all is very sincere.

That's the reason why God holds us all so dear.

It is wonderful got our congregation to be standing
in the gateway of eternity.

So if you are looking for somewhere that you
feel like you belong.

Adopt Covington Church as your Church home.

We are serving the Lord with pride.

Me

God placed me upon this Earth.

I had no idea what I was worth.

Within me there is a light that shines so bright.

That it guides my way through the cold still night.

As I adventure within this lost huge world.

I find that my gift is like a pearl.

It is as precious as it can possibly be.

Sent down from Heaven and appointed unto me.

The words that I write can set souls free.

Thus making mankind hunger for me.

The words tantalizes people thoughts and
mesmerizes their minds.

Setting the captives free thus leading the blind.

I remember the things that I use to do. How I went
through life not knowing who.

Who I was or from where I came.

Always looking for someone in whom
I can place the blame.

Much was said and much was done.

Through it all a lesson was learned.

He is in I and I am in He.

His glorious light shines within me.

My path was laid before I came.

Even before I had a name.

Even before I was born, the victory I had already won.

God made the Earth and God made the sea.

God put his spirit inside of me.

So I thank you Father for who I am, and keep me close to

Jesus the Lamb.

I am a shining light for all to see.

I am of Him for He lives in me.

The Champ

I am the Champ living my life for thee.
That is the title that God gave me.
In the eyes of The Lord I walk the walk.
Each and every day I talk the talk.
I'm knocking out sicknesses and mutilating sin.
I'm feeding the people so they can win.
Satan is big but he is not bad.
I'm taking back the souls that he thought that he had.
I'm preaching the gospel here and there.
People are being saved everywhere.
The full amour of God is all that you need.
Then have faith the size of a mustard seed.
Satan has absolutely no power over you.
S he can't tell you what to do.
God's word is sharp as a two edged sword.
Study it daily to reap its reward.
It is all of the training that you need.
To grow into a champion breed.
I am the champ and this I know.
When I step in the ring Satan won't show.
He knows that he can't last one round.
Every time that he get up I knock him back down.
You can be a champion too.
Just let our Savior Jesus train you.

Winner

I'm being the best woman of God that I can possibly be.
When the Bible speaks of a virtuous woman
it's talking about me.
When it speaks about her standards it makes me feel proud.
My ways are just like hers standing out in a crowd.
From the beginning of the day to the end of the night.
Everything that I do is honest and right.
My children love me and call me blessed.
Even though Satan attacks me I still pass the test.
My husband will sit within the Holy Gate.
I live a holy life and for Jesus I will wait.
As Heaven is up high and Earth is below.
The compassion of the Lord is one thing that I know.
He is better to us that we are to our self.
As long as I got King Jesus I don't need anybody else.
I am proud to be who I am in God.
And no matter what happens He will always
have my heart.
No one knows when He is coming back again.
But whenever he does I know that I will win.
A Crown in Heaven.

Grace

God is good all the time.

Even when we are out of line.

Even when we are doing our wrong.

He guides our path and keeps us strong.

Our sinful nature is very weak.

He allows us to reach our highest peak.

And just when we have gone astray.

He lights our path and shows us the way.

He is always right by our side.

When we are in need he always provide.

He knows that our love for him is pure.

But our sinful nature can't endure.

He knows that we are in need of a Host.

So he sends us His precious Holy Ghost.

It's up to us to let him in.

He gives us grace so we can win.

Against sin . . .

Host

I am your host let me in.

You cannot win against sin.

All by yourself you won't prevail.

You'll only send yourself to Hell.

I am here for you to make you strong.

I will teach you how to leave them sins alone.

Just do the things that I tell you to do.

Then watch your life become brand new.

You have powers that you do not know.

Power to make the Devil go.

Go back to hell from whence he came.

Your soul is at stake so this is no game.

How long must I wait?

What are you going to do?

When Jesus comes back you will be through.

An Angel

We don't know what could have happened;
we know not what went wrong.
For this unfortunate incident has sent Tiffany home.
There is nothing that we can say or
anything that we can do.
We wish that this was a dream with
no chance of coming true.
But we must face the fact that she is forever gone.
The best thing about the situation is that
we know she went home.
Home in the hands of God is the best place to be.
Safe from Harms way to spend eternity.
Although the pain is great and too hard to bear.
One thing that we do know is that she is
getting the best of care.
So you don't have to worry and you don't have to cry.
Your Tiffany is now an Angel in God's infinite sky.

May God Bless, Comfort and keep you all.

Don't Worry

Pastor you don't have to worry, your help is on the way.
Jesus is your Hero and he's here to save the day.
He has granted you salvation to save your very soul.
His precious Holy Spirit is worth more than solid gold.
He gave you wisdom, knowledge and understanding to
help you in every way.
Then he gives you guardian angels to
protect you every day.
He awakes you every morning and lay you down at night.
All the sins that you have ever committed have
been taken off your back.
He feeds you when you are hungry and
gives you what you need.
All you have to do is to follow your Bishop's lead.
Jesus showed us what to do when
he walked upon this land.
There is nothing on this earth that Jesus didn't command.
So Bishop try not to worry.
Your help is on the way.
Just cast all your cares upon Jesus.
And keep doing what the Bible says.

Happy Birthday Jesus

The world was dark then came the son.
The life that we know had just begun.
All the sins that we had committed were washed away.
For Jesus was born to save the day.
Jesus was born to let us in.
He gave us the strength so that we could win.
He is the gift that God gave to us.
The only thing that we have to do is trust.
Trust in Jesus with all of our heart.
Then believe that he is the true Son of God.
So if your life is in darkness just follow the son.
Thro Jesus the victory is already won.
Jesus is the reason for the season.
Merry Christmas

A Miracle

Oh what a holy night, the sound of Angels fills the Earth.
Let us all get our lives right, for Heaven we are worth.
Christmas is the birthday of our King;
He was born in a manger.
So Hark, the Herald let us all sing, along with the Angels.
It's Christmas time once again, so compassion
we all must give.
Send a gift to a friend; Jesus gave his life so we could live.
The first Noel is a very good song that we all should sing.
For we are all very blessed that God gave us a King.
Born in the flesh, as we are so we can know his pain.
He was found by following a star now our
lives are not the same.
A precious miracle was given to us.
Now all we have to do is trust.
Jesus was born for all mankind.
I am so glad that I have made him mine.
Jesus is the reason for the Christmas season!
Thanks for showing us the way.

Heaven

I can only imagine what heaven look like.
I heard that it's a breathtaking sight.
I know that just seeing it will take my breath away.
I will stand there speechless with no understandable
words to say.
I can only imagine the solid gold streets.
And the river of mild and honey where everyone meet.
There will be no sorrow; there will be no pain.
There will be no cripple; there will be no lame.
There will be no sickness; there will be no death.
We will all have plenty and an abundance of wealth.
I can only imagine many mansions in a house.
Where the cat will love and get along with the mouse.
We don't have to imagine, just live the right way.
Then you will get to see God's heaven one day.
You will see the throne sitting behind a sea of glass.
Then you'll be able to say that you're free at last.

My Love

There are a lot of things that I really do adore.
You are embedded in my heart deep within the core.
Out of all of the beautiful colors my favorite is green.
It is an indication of life especially in the spring.
I really love Pineapples are great and so unique.
They freshens the air around us and taste so very sweet.
A Camaro is beautiful and truly the car of my dream.
Just sitting behind the wheel in one makes me
feel like a queen.
A pink tulip is the most amazing flower that there is.
When the raindrops fall of it they resemble tears.
These are some of the things that I really do love.
They remind me of you in whom I often think of.
I think of just how much that I sincerely love you.
Thus I am looking forward to the day that we
vow to say we do.
What God has placed together will stand and never fall.
We will always love each other more than
you love Basketball.
I look forward to being your wife.

Bonded

There is a bond that exists between a Father and a Son.
In reality it's an inseparable bond.
There is a connection that no one knows.
A strong man neglect to let it show.
A father loves his son in each and every way.
He corrects him so that he will be successful one day.
The father disciplines the son just to make him strong.
So that one day the son can stand on his own.
Sometimes the son doesn't understand.
He knows not the reason nor does he know the plan.
You might have gone through some things that no one knows.
With your mighty strength you didn't let it show.
You went on your way, you made the day.
Now there is nothing that no one can say.
Sometimes when we lose we actually win.
The strength to succeed will come in the end.
Although sometimes you may have gone astray.
You remembered the lessons and found your way.
Always be thankful for the lessons that you were taught.
They helped to conquer the battles that you fought.
The son loves his father. The Father loves his son.
The two will always b bonded as one.
For I am in you and you are in me.
We'll be together forever throughout eternity.

Devotion

A devoted man of God is more powerful
than any words can ever say.
It means that you are walking with the Father
in each and every way.
It means that you trust in Jesus from the
bottom of your heart.
You are working for the king and doing your part.
You are in his perfect will in everything that you do.
This battle is not yours for He is fighting for you.
His word is as sharp as a two-edged sword.
Thus breaking the yoke and filling the void.
An Apostle job is to travel the land, preaching
the gospel to all that he can.
A Pastor's job is to feed the sheep, ensuring that
salvation is worthy to keep.
A prophet job is to prophesy a judgment call. Yield to his
message least you fall.
Sometimes we don't know what to do. We know that God
will pull us through.
Sometimes we don't know what to say. It's not an option
God will have his way.
By the blood of Jesus Satan can't stand.

God has anointed you and blessed your hands.
He has given you wisdom that you do not know.
He will always show you which way to go.
He will guide you with his very own hand. You may travel
all across the land.
The miracles of old have never gone away.
The victory is your, you can claim it today.
Remember that God is always by your side.
As He did for Elijah, He will definitely provide.

Change

Spiritual Reality is what we need.

It is the only way that our soul feeds.

Feast on the Word of God to Grown Big and Strong.

Being endowed by the Spirit so we can stand alone.

Standing firm in our faith, never to fall.

Strong in the word and answering God's call.

Heaven is high and Earth is below.

The thoughts of the Lord we will never know.

For our thoughts are no His and His are not ours.

God is the Supreme infinite power.

He holds the world in His hand.

We must submit and follow his plan.

Hell is empty because the Demons are here.

Change your life for the end is near.

Anti-Drug Festival 2005

We all claim to be concerned about the world.
Here is a chance to save a boy or a girl.
They are faced with dangers where they can't win.
We can nip it in the bud before it begins.
Our children are our future and that we all know.
We must show them which way to go.
Saying no to drugs is a message to them all.
If we don't intervene they definitely will fall.
They have no idea what they are up against.
Drugs will destroy them in a synch.
It's up to us to show them the way.
That drugs, crime and alcohol don't pay.
We must join forces to win this war on drugs.
Our whole environment is controlled by thugs.
Mr. Crack is dominating all over the land.
He is the Dragon in this brutal slaying.
He doesn't care about me and He doesn't care about you.
If he gets our children they will be through.
No life, no future, another burden to the world.
Another lost soul, poor boy, and poor girl!
Support Anti—Drug Festival 2005.
By stomping out drugs and keeping their dream alive.

Ray Hagin

Mr. Knock out drugs is here to stay.

Ray Hagin will show our kids the way.

He's knocking out drugs here and there.

He's cleaning up our communities everywhere.

From city to city and coast to coast.

Ray is the one that the dealers fear the most.

They are the ones that he intends to reveal.

Before they can make their very next deal.

Without the dealers there would be no drugs.

Besides the dealers are nothing but thugs.

Thugs don't care about anything. So Ray is inviting

them into the ring.

Knock them out Ray, save the day! Make

them throw those drugs away.

They are just looking for an easy way out.

To make some money and to get some clout.

They prey on the weak and everyone else.

But we know that they are actually weak themselves.

Living in vain, hoping for gain, while driving the whole

world completely insane.

Drugs promote violence, mayhem and crime.

Drug addict will take a life for a dime.

But have no fear, Ray is here to stay!

Knocking out drugs every day.

Let us all work side by side, to make illegal

drugs take a ride.

This world will be a better pace.

If Ray knock all of the drugs dealers in the outer space.

Elvis

This poem is for someone who is special to me.
He opened my eyes and made me see.
He told me that I could conquer the world.
While inspiring every man, woman, boys and girls.
You told me that I could be a star.
And that my gift would take me very far.
You believed in me a long time ago.
You have more faith in me than I will ever know.
You want me to win and I know that you do.
When that day comes I won't forget you.
When that day comes I want you by my side.
Then we both can taste success with pride.
Where ever I am I want you to be.
What I look at I want you to see.
If the world was mine I would give half to you.
And I bet that you would know what to do.
Please stay as you are for you are a true Man of God.
Keep his spirit locked deep within your heart.
Your mother gave you the greatest gift of all.
With the love that you have you will never fall.
Elvis I thank God for you a true friend to the end.

Saint Paul

Saint Paul AME is a church that is one of a kind.
It started over 100 years ago before any of our time.
In the home of Sister Mary Larey back in 1870.
For she and her husband Elder Larey lived in this community.
She organized a prayer meeting right in her very own home.
Once a week they worshiped but it didn't last too long.
The room was much too small and couldn't accommodate
the growing crowd.
The Blue-Black Speller and Turner Catechism
were taught very proud.
She commissioned her daughter Lizzie for
Sunday school to teach.
The mission grew so rapidly that they
needed a minister to preach.
Brother Sipio Robinson was sent to pastor by Reverend Pack.
Not everything was in order and on the right track.
Sister Larey was an African Methodist
which is what we are today.
Elder Larey was a Missionary Baptist and
taught a different way.

Both congregations rapidly grew
while using the same place.
But they decided to separate the two to
keep peace among the race.
A saint call Brother London Armstrong
bought a piece of land.
He gave the AMC a piece to build a church to stand.
In 1872 Reverend I. N. Fitzpatrick was the
first pastor of Saint Paul.
He server for only 2 years thus leading the long haul.
A long haul of preachers Saint Paul has seen come and go.
In 1985 the finances took a blow.
In 1989 marked a year of drastic change.
A dynamic 23 year old preacher whom everyone thought
was strange.
Pastor Terrence Renard Gray definitely held his own!
While teaching the word of God
He taught them to be strong.
Delighted, Excited and Ignited while
on fire with the Holy Ghost.
Bishop John Hurst Adams must have known that Terrence
would rock the coast.
Saint Paul has grown tremendously and
is still growing today.
It is equipped to accommodate us all
in our own special way.
With numerous outreach ministries
Saint Paul can hold its own.

If we keep our eyes to the hills we can do no wrong.

135 years is how long that we have been around.

Saint Paul will still exist when we are all in the ground.

So let's continue to grow for we are not yet done,

We all had a mighty fight getting to 2501.

Saint Paul is a church known for its faith . . .

Hallelujah

Hallelujah is the highest praise.
Just by saying the word you can receive God's grace.
By saying Hallelujah you can bless yourself.
By doing the will of God you can receive much wealth.
Jarvis is a man that loves the Lord.
He is just like David after God's own heart.
The Lord is his shepherd and He should not want.
If God says not to do it Jarvis don't!
God allows him to lie down in a pasture that's green.
He once was a baby but now he's been weaned.
Hallelujah is the word that he says all of the time.
His honor to God is truly divine.
God leads him beside still waters and restored his soul.
One day he will receive a crown that's gold.
He shouts Hallelujah in the valley of death.
Whenever he is sick, God restored his health.
His head is anointed and his cup runneth over.
It's like he possesses a four leafed clover.
Hallelujah has taken him a long, long, way.
He makes it a habit to say it every day.
He shouts Hallelujah in all kinds of weather.
In the house of the Lord He will dwell forever

Let us all say Hallelujah and Amen . . .

Tomorrow

Our leaders for tomorrow are right here today.
Even our president had to start this way.
First he had to go to school.
To learn all that he could while following the rules.
He has to also do what was right.
To get along with others and try not to fight.
Then he had to do his best.
To try and be number one while never settling for less.
Our leaders for tomorrow are right here today!
What will you be when it comes your way?
You can be a doctor, a lawyer, a nurse of fly planes.
Whatever you do success is the same.
So be the best at what you are.
That is the only way that you can go far.

Love

Being overwhelmed with emotions, and overjoyed by
your sight.
Looking forward to the day, I can't wait until tonight.
I have a feeling deep within that can't be explained.
I am trying to control my emotions to keep
from going insane.
Love . . .
It's so deep that it cuts to the bone.
I'm tantalized by the thought, I wonder is it wrong?
Putting others feelings first, neglecting yourself.
Not caring about tomorrow or anything else.
Love
Is it reality or is a dream?
Sometimes situations are not what they seem.
Should you expect the same love that you so humbly give?
Without true love is there a reason to live?
Love . . .
Associating, conversating, negotiating while anticipating.
Being mesmerized, tranquilized, domitized and traumatized.
Being irritated emancipated, proclamated and aggravated.
Hypnotized, pulverized, penalized and ostracized.

Love and being in love with someone that you love.
What is Love?

Mighty Mother

God made woman just for man.
But He also had a divine plane.
He knew that man could not survive
without a woman by his side.
He put all authority in her hands.
For she was blessed to populate the land.
As long as we live there will never be another.
Who is more valuable than a mother?
A Mother knows how to love, a Mother is sweet.
A mother is personal and very unique.
By a mother we all entered into this world.
Even Jesus was born from a sweet innocent girl.
So Mothers this day is dedicated to you.
You always know just what to do.
You always know just what to say.
The smartest thing to do is to stay out of your way.
Our life would not exist if it were not for you.
So our love will always be faithful and true.
We sincerely love you forever and beyond.
And you will always be second to none.
God created woman as a blessing to the world.
But a mother is more precious than diamonds and pearls.
Your mother is the mightiest person in the land.
She gave you life, now isn't that grand?

Free Father

Here it is fellas this is our day. Nobody has anything to say.

There are still things that they want us to do.

I am still tired what about you?

Since its Father's day we should say, "Leave us alone and

let us have our way"!

Give us a week to let us do what we do.

We will catch up on some fishing and hunting too.

We won't take out the trash or mow the lawn.

We will sleep and eat from dusk to dawn.

We will just recline and watch TV all day.

You can do all of the work and we'll collect the pay.

You can even pretend that we are not at home.

Just make sure that the children leave us alone.

Please make sure that we have something to eat.

And when you get time will you massage our feet.

This is a Father's Day dream that will never come true.

If it did we would definitely be through.

The only way that we can be saved is residing in a

covered grave.

So while we are here we are a gift to the world.
We are chosen over diamonds and pearls.
They need us daily in each and every way.
And we need them more than words can say.
We thank you for recognizing us upon this special day.
But for 24 hours please let us have our way.
Happy Father's Day to all of the devoted Fathers . . .

Guardian

Carl's precious soul has been committed to the hands of
God.
There is no need to feel dismayed for everyone did their part.
There is no need to be sad because you
did all that you could do.
Carl knew that you loved him dearly and that
he really loved you too.
It is the will of God to lead his children home.
Residing in His Heavenly Kingdom is where we all belong.
God has given him to fly low and high.
He is free at last and will possibly stop by.
Now He's a Guardian Angel, protecting you from above.
Watching over you Patsy and showering you with love.
You will never be alone in all that you do.
For your Guardian Angel Husband is watching over you.
Carl was blessed to have a Spiritual family
standing by his side.
To lead him home to Jesus by accepting
Salvation with pride.

Carl will certainly be missed by people great and small.
But his lovely wife Patsy will miss him most of all.
So he doesn't want us to worry and
He doesn't want us to cry.
For he is blessed to be with God in the infinite sky.

The Egg theory

We as humans are somewhat like the product of an egg. Being locked and cultivated within, where we are protected and guarded by a source greater than ourselves. Our world is so fragile, which makes us vulnerable to society as a whole. The slightest fall could result in a fatality, unless of course the surface in which we fall is cushioned and soft enough so that we can sustain the impact.

The point of the matter is that the egg has a destiny that is basically determined by its master unless some significant source of the product or its ancestors changes its destiny.

In essence the point of the parable is that some eggs are nursed. This process of nurturing allows it to hatch and be manifested into a beautiful living chick that has been allotted the precious gift of life, thus destituting the probability to further its generation in a different world.

As we know all eggs don't hatch. The unfortunate ones are collected, packaged and shipped to supermarkets all over the world where their destiny lies on someone breakfast plate.

This without a doubt brings forth their demise and ends their world.

We find ourselves in the same situation. Our destiny has already been predetermined considering of course that fact that we don't we change our life by not following and accepting Christ as our savior which will lead to eternal life.

The children of God will hatch upon the end of the world. This will allow them to delight themselves with life in the new world. Whereas the children of wrath will unfortunately find themselves cracked and burned upon a hot surface which will forever end their world. There they will find themselves being someone's breakfast. That someone is the Devil.

Therefore I encourage you to be a beautiful, desirable, healthy egg so that you can prove to your master that you are worthy of furthering your existence. If so you will be nursed and allowed to hatch into a beautiful chick into a new and innovative world.

Otherwise you may find yourself packed and shipped somewhere where your world will end in tragedy . . . . FRIED HARD.

Think about it . . . Try God!

Sacred Center

Everything belongs to God in each and every way.
It doesn't matter how we feel He always have his say.
It doesn't matter what we do we can't do nothing right.
Even though we may try hard with
all of our strength and might.
God is the ultimate judge who judges us
when we are wrong.
We are grateful for his directions that always lead us home.
All glory belongs to God no matter what price we pay.
Things that we consider priceless,
He will throw them all away.
Some of the things that we love so very much may have
gotten tainted having a worldly touch.
Rejection is simply direction, showing us another way.
It may also be protection which keeps us from going astray.
Blessed is Allen Temple for God has his eyes on you.
He is pleased with your worship so
He's giving you something new.
Now you can start all over and this time make it right.
Keep your temple sacred for it is holy in his sight.

The new Allen Temple AME will be known
from miles away.
But let us all be reminded, least we'll forget that awful day.
Nothing is ever promise, but God is in control.
Our brand new worship center will be more
sacred than precious gold.
God has truly Blessed Allen Temple AME . . .

A Change

Uprooted from the chains of oppression,
bound in a world of shame.
A beacon of light is glowing, ordained to make a change.
From the poverty stricken streets of Chicago,
to the steps of Harvard Law.
We would all be amazed at some of the things He saw.
We would all stand in awe at some of the
things that he did.
Let's take this magic moment to let Obama do our bid.
Obama is indeed a Blackman, but that's not really the case.
His political point of view is what kept him in the race.
The things that he talks about and
the things that he likes to do.
Makes crowds scream and shout plus
he's looking out for you.
I'm voting for Barak Obama he's the best man for the job.
America has had her share of presidents
that only stole and robbed.
Now it's your time to vote, step up and take a stand.
Let's flood the pool with numbers all across the land.
Barak Obama is your man! He will get the job done!
Just by getting this far, we have already won.

We are fighting a losing battle, each and every day.
The war in the Middle East is taking our children away.
We can't continue to fight and live our lives the same.
We don't have many options, so let's vote to
make a change.
Now that we have a chance let's take it all the way.
The only thing that we have to do is use our vote to say.

Angela

We all have a title in which we call a name.
Some our namely title will help us gain some fame.

Is for angelic, which you are in being.
For you are destined to be a queen

N—is for nice, for that's what you are.
Your politeness will take to places
Afar
G—Is for grand. The finale of them all.
Your abundance of beauty makes
You stand tall.

E—Is for Elegance, with your own unique style.
There is nothing more charming than
To see your beautiful smile.

L—Is for love, that's stored in your heart.
It's a special kind of love that no one
can depart.

Is for always that I will love you.
If it wasn't for you, I wouldn't
Know what to do.

Your name is of Fame so wear it well.
You may be a legend one day only time can tell.

Blackman Ineffectual Annihilation

In this vast worldly contraption of technologized commercing and economics, the African American is without a doubt presently economically ineffectually annihilated. To be view in a category such as this in the areas of business is a sign of inadequacy. Entrepreneurship, chain stores, and conglomerate giants are at an all time high. The black race was not labeled in this term by any other race. They merely earned this title by being insufficient and dependent on ever other race to provide for their goods and services that actually safeguard their existence. They have no one else to blame but themselves for being the worst financially invariable, insufficient race on the planet Earth.

All across the United States of America their economic status follow the same pattern. They do not own businesses which results to them not being in control of their own communities.

The do not own grocery stores, convenient stores, services stations, department stores, hospitals, banks or any other lucrative business.

They depend 90% on the businesses and establishments of other races top provide their every need. The 10% of (BOB) Black Owned Businesses is not supported by their very own race which leaves them void and defeated.

The Black dollar is the single most powerful entity in the capitalistic market. Unfortunately, it is divided between the other races and distributed throughout the globe thus leaving their very own neighborhoods drained, dilapidated and destitute.

God forbids! If all other races refused to serve the African American they will find themselves living in a dark and primitive world.

However there is no alarm or need to worry about them boycotting businesses but we know that the economy could not survive without the black dollar.

African American is capable of doing and owning anything that any other race can, perhaps better. What then is the problem? Why don't blacks form an alliance to own businesses and take charge of their communities?

It is purely pathetic that Indians from as far as the Middle East travel thousands of miles to own and operate convenient stores in the heart and core of the black communities. They proudly and boldly prey upon their communities. Unfortunately, they are welcomed with open arms and full pockets.

African American as a people needs to stop this madness!

They need to find a way to take charge of their own communities.

Start an Alliance to build (BOB) Black Own Businesses, symbolize it, enterprise it, then internationalize it, so we can be self-sufficient and independent, depending upon ourselves and no one else now and beyond.

Or we can do nothing like we always have and find ourselves being manipulated and violated until we are totally economically annihilated . . .

Reality

Dr. Martin Luther King had a beautiful dream.

His dream was to let freedom ring.

Let it ring from the mountains; let it ring from the sea.

Let it ring globally, making the whole world free.

His dream has become a reality. We all are living together, happy and free.

We are the proof that his dream came true. Just take a look at me and you.

We work, praise, and do everything, under the sun. This is evidence that the battle is won.

We are getting along the way we should.

We are caring and sharing the same neighborhood.

We even dine together, feasting side by side. Wearing our perspective color with pride.

We are respecting each other in each and every way. If he could see us now, what would he say?

On this freedom ride we are being our self. Living in peace and Harmony with everyone else.

We have a freedom of choice and a freedom of speech.

And our goal can be whatever we choose to reach.

Many have been born and many have died. But we are all partaking this American Pride.

Oh how I wish that Dr. King could see. Us living together
in blissful harmony.
I wish that he could see us together praising God. Walking
hand in hand on one accord.
The past is behind us; that we cannot change.
But society as we know it has been has been totally
rearranged.
We thank you Dr. King, yes your dream came true. For
freedom is ringing and we owe it to you.
Yes we thank you Dr.King for that wonderful dream.
Now working together we can do anything.
It's truly a beautiful sight for us all to see. Dr. King, your
dream is reality.
We all thank you for making this world a better place . . .

Arisen

I'm so glad that the Angel said that Jesus Christ
Had risen from the dead.
Our Lord Jesus was a present to the world.
He is more precious than diamonds and pearls.
In the beginning was the word and the word
was with God.
Sent down from Heaven, giving us a brand new start.
Wrapped in swaddling clothing, born in a manger.
Proclaimed to Man by God's Mighty Holy Angels.
Jesus is the reason for any season.
The kingdom is ours if we don't commit treason.
Confess him with our mouth and believe him in our heart.
It's the only way that we can be with God.
Jesus has gone to where we will be.
He is constantly building Mansions for you and me.
Birds have nests and foxes have dens.
By trusting in Jesus we all can win.
So let's be encouraged each and every day.
Read God's word and do what it say.

After 3 days in Hell they rolled back the stone.

They peeked inside and Jesus was gone.

I'm so glad that the Angels said that Jesus Christ had risen from the dead.

Come all you who are thirsty, come to the water . . .

Isaiah 55:1

Racist

Believe it or not racism lies within.
Inside of our heart is where it all begins.
It has to be nurtured and allowed to grow.
Where would it end? How far will it go?
It has no core for racism is blind.
There is no place to draw the line.
What color are you? What color is God?
What color is blood and the human heart?
We all breathe the very same air.
The Earth's resources are ours to share.
You inhale the air that I exhale for the core of life.
Why should there be controversy and strife?
There is only one way that this world can be strong.
Which is working together and getting along.
Racism is a disease where no one is immune.
It starts in your heart and your life it consumes.
It is easy to stop racism where it begins.
Just clean your heart and let love come in.
It has nothing to do with anyone else.
It is a condition that we all need to purge within ourselves.

Profound Love

I confess my love to you and tell how much I care.
Where you are I will be right there.
We are true lovers who walk hand in hand.
Dedicating our lives and living out God's plan.
We were born as one but we shouldn't stay that way.
I need you love each and every day.
When I emerge from my sleep and open my eyes.
I take one look at you and my temperature rise.
I am always in Heaven with you by my side.
I am honored that you wear my name with pride.
I can't phantom living live without you.
I have no idea what I will do.
I have no idea where I will go.
Maybe it's because I love you so.
I can escape to the mountains.
I can sail the seven seas.
But there is no place that I would rather be.
So there is no need for me to run away.
Your heart is my home and that's where I will stay.

Believe me when I say that I am still in love with you . . .

Greatest Love

Mother's day is everyday but we celebrate it once a year.
We all know that if it wasn't for Mothers
we wouldn't be here.
To all Mothers you are honored for you
gave life to the world.
There is nothing more precious to a mother
to their baby boy girl.
There is nothing more precious to a baby than its mother.
It's a special place in our heart that
can't be filled by another.
A mother is more precious than anything
on this massive earth.
No price could ever be put on how much you are worth.
I know that you are the best of the
best in each and every way.
I pray that God will bless you abundantly
upon this special day.
Although you are stern don't ever change
the way that you are.

It is the only way that you can help me go far.
It is Mother's day and you have a reason to
stand proud and tall.
To you dear Mother you are the greatest love of all.
Happy Mother's day
I love you

Next

Stop, think and listen to what I have to say.

HIV and Aids is here and unfortunately here to stay.

How did it start?

Where will it end?

Is it a plague for our immoral sin?

It has no color.

It has no name,

It encompass the rich and the poor the same.

There is no place to run and no place to hide.

If you put yourself at risk, prepare for the ride.

Millions of people are being infected every day.

Because they placed themselves in Aids harm way.

The medical profession is trying their best.

To stomp out the plague and save the rest.

So protect yourself in all that you do.

The next Aids victim could be you.

Practice safe sex . . .

Extra Ordinary People

We're just ordinary people, looking to God for
which way to go.
Because we ordinary people, we need to
learn to take it slow.
We look to you for what we need.
Yes, we need you very much.
In life, we all would like to succeed.
So we got have your touch.
Touch us with your wisdom, your knowledge and
understanding.
We are realize that we sometime be so very demanding.
We are indeed the future, to run the world that you live in.
By giving us your knowledge is the only way
that we can win.
So help us to win tomorrow, by teaching us how today.
We will all be lost if you don't show us the way.
If you neglect to guide us, there is nothing
that you can say.
It would not be a pleasant sight to see us go astray.

So make life easy for yourself by supporting us in this cause.
We are pleading for your support and guidance,
don't let us be lost
We are just ordinary people, trying to walk in authority.
God always use ordinary people and I hope that he use me.
To do extraordinary things

Victorious

Don't ever give up.
You can win.
Condition yourself before you begin.
Condition your mind to have faith in yourself.
If you succeed you may encounter wealth.
Put God first in everything that you do.
For its Satan job to defeat you.
We know that he is busy each and every day.
He'll do anything to chase happiness away.
No matter how hard a task maybe.
It's easy to claim a victory.
Just don't give up.
Give it all you got.
Before you know it you'll be on top.

Heavy

You can't lift it up but you can pick it up.
Sometimes it may seem that you don't understand.
Even though the answer lies right in your hand.
Ideas are constantly in demand.
You pick them up but you can't lift them up.
Sometimes things may seem too hard.
However it's easy to pick them apart.
Use your head and think smart.
Then you'll conquer it from the start.
You can pick it up but you can't lift it up.
Love on the horizon all vibrant and new.
Bringing in happiness and chasing away the blue.
So overjoyed not knowing what to do.
You can lift it up but you can't pick it up.
Conversations get heavy as hills are steep.
The wisdom is wise as oceans are deep within words there
lies mystery to seek.
You can pick it up but you can't lift it up.

Madness

In the mist of much madness, why would anyone
want to steal my joy?
Why would someone want to steal my joy,
on a day that's very hot?
Do anyone want to see me happy? A smile is all I got.
Why would someone want to steal my joy, when the
world is on my shoulder?
I feel like I have been crushed by a huge, gigantic boulder.
Why should someone steal my joy when
I'm trying so very hard?
To leave the burdens of the world to Almighty God.
Do you want to see me happy?
Do you want to see me smile?
Then why are you treating me like an
estranged demonic child?
I'm trying to beat the game of life by being a model man.
But every time I see the light, you block it if you can.
I don't have to worry. Everything will be all right.
God will come in a hurry to change the
darkness into the light.

So refuse to worry, for you'll never steal my joy.
Unto God's children, this world is just a toy.
So before you steal my joy, I know just what to do . . .
Just find my own place in space so I won't
encounter you . . .

Help

Help someone by helping yourself.
You're in control of none else.
Each has himself only to teach.
For we each must set a goal to reach.
What can you do for someone else?
If within your life you have been left.
In need of someone else to help yourself.
How can you help someone else?
Strive for perfection and strive above.
Conquer the goals that you have dreamed of.
Live the life that you want to live.
Obtain much substance, only then can you give.
The more things that you acquire for yourself.
The more you can do for someone else.
God above stands above all.
He holds our finances until we call.
He will provide whatever we need.
He fills the void and feeds the greed.
It's a blessing to be able to help someone else.
But the first thing that you must do is help yourself.

Happy Anniversary

Pastor we proudly celebrate this Anniversary just for you.
We are very pleased in the things that you do.
We are so satisfied with the things that you say.
We are truly blessed to have you leading the way.
A great man of God is who you are.
We know that you will take our congregation far.
For you are the Sheppard and we are the sheep.
Constantly leading us to the pasture to reap.
Here in this church is the place to be.
Just come and visit and you will see.
You are welcome to be a part of us.
We worship our God and in Jesus we trust.
We have just gotten started so we are still small.
But our spirit is bouncing off the wall.
The children are our future and that you know.
We must teach them which way to go.
We are proud to have you teaching what you saw.
We are right here with you in this war.
We are worshipping God hand in hand.
Right by your side we will proudly stand.
We all want you to know that we are very proud of you.
Just keep on doing the things that you do.

Hall of Famer

Tony was the type of person that loved everyone.
He always gave everything his all until the battle was won.
He loved his fiancé' Shirley more that we'll ever know.
To us all it was a mystery as to why he chose to go.
He loved and provided to Tony Jr. and Nathaniel
in each and every way.
We know that he will watch over them
each and every day.
Home Depot was truly blessed to have him on their side.
He always had a smile on his face while serving his
customers with pride.
He was a quiet calculated person with a glow upon his face.
Whenever he walked into a room He illuminated
the entire place.
From LSU to Auburn he loved the Tigers so.
I can still hear his yelling, "Go Tigers go".
NASCAR was a favorite, Tony Stewart was his man.
Cajun foods, Hot Wheels and bottle tops
were all in his plan.
We will all miss Tony dearly and
we don't know what to say.

Everyone will eventually leave this world but we don't
know which way.
God please have mercy on Tony and caress
him in your arms.
He was a blessing to us all and never did any harm.
Make him a supreme Angel to watch us from above.
Let his light shine upon us while emminating his love.
Perhaps he wasn't satisfied while giving us his all.
Perhaps you could have hasten his desire and made him
answer your call.
Tony has left a legacy to carry forth his name.
Tony with your family and store 0881
you are in our Hall of Fame.

Homelessness

To find yourself homeless is really not a shame.
Sometime you may not be the only one to blame.
Something may have happen where you had no control.
It is not your fault that the forces of nature
decided to take a toll.
It is true that we all must live from day to day.
We never know what might happen or
what might come our way.
We will never know what really lie ahead.
We may be honored or we may be misled.
The majority of people are one step away.
From being homeless the very next day.
One step away from owning their dream.
And one step away from losing everything.
A fire, a storm job closing and such.
Anything can happen there is so very much.
We must put our trust in God in all of the
things that we do.
He is the only one who can pull us through.
Birds have nests and foxes have dens.
By trusting in Jesus we will always win.
The war on Homelessness.

Living

Never give up on life no matter what you do.
It is a gift from God that your parents gave you.
Always honor your parents with the life that you live.
For they have given more to you than
anyone could ever give.
There will be times when you know not what to do.
Never lose focus on those who truly loves you.
There will be some days where you
know not where to begin.
Those same bad dreadful days will help you in the end.
It is a blessing to be the parent to a little boy or girl.
We never stop to realize that we are indeed their world.
We can do no wrong in their loving eager eyes.
Their world would be destroyed if we met our demise.
Always trust in God for He will make a way.
He always speaks for us when
we don't have anything to say.
Rejection is direction and sometimes protection.
Sometimes it's our fault if we fail to do inspection.
You are truly loved much more that you'll ever know.
You'll destroy all of our lives if you chose to go.
A lot of things will change; I will never be the same.

Where did I go wrong? Am I the one to blame?
Listen, learn, love and learn, while always
protecting your heart.
There is nothing in this world more important
than our God.

Than to love the life that He gave you to live . . .

Commitment

Thomas, this poem is just for you.
It maybe advising you on what to do.
It may even help you to get a brand new start.
I truly do love you from the death of my heart.
I truly love you and I think that you know.
But I think that it's time for me to let you go.
I think that it may be time for me to go my own way.
I am beginning to run out of words to say.
You take my love for granted and I feel no respect.
I really can't continue this life of neglect.
So I am forced to do what I got to do.
For the record it's not just to prove a point to you.
It feels like I have finally opened my eyes.
I was in denial but now I do realize.
It is not fair to me to be in love all by myself.
I might as well protect my heart and love someone else.
Thomas I love you more that you'll ever know.
I don't want to throw what we have out of the door.
I don't want our relationship to end this way.
But it's up to you so what can I say.
I am leaving it up to you so what will it be?
Let's commit together or we can go free.

Confession

You are very special; you make me feel brand new.

I think that I must admit it perhaps I love you too.

I feel that you are straight and as sweet as you can be.

You are the kind of person that I want to be with me.

I have been through a lot and it's really hard to explain.

It's a possibility that I may not ever be the same.

I admit that I am sacred and don't know what to do.

And I keep wondering if I should give my heart to you.

Will you take care of my heart if I put it on the line?

I am not the type that will share I only want what's mine.

Can I trust in you is something that I need to know.

Only then will I be comfortable enough

to let my feeling show.

Your confession of love to me and the promises you made.

Makes me look forward to the things you have conveyed.

Will you take care of my heart? Do you know what to do?

I don't know where to start so I am leaving it up to you.

Now that you have my attention, where do we go

from here?

Here is a consolation to the situation, "I love you when
you're near".
Even though I am apprehensive I am
willing to take a stand.
Now I am leaving it up to you, do you
want to be my man?
A confession is the key so what will it be . . .

Happy Birthday Jarvis

Happy Birthday Jarvis today is your day.
We might just let you have some things your way.
We might let you do some things that you want to do.
That is only because we truly do love you.
I love you more that you will ever know.
With my actions I always let it show.
I sincerely love you in each and every way.
I love you more than any words can say.
You are a wonderful person with a very good heart.
You are the kind of person that is set aside for God.
You can't do the things that other people do.
God's eyes and hands are always on you.
He always walks beside you everywhere you go.
Whenever you go wrong He will always let you know.
Indeed it is difficult and I know that you don't understand.
But you are a child of God and part of his master plan.
You were tried by fire and fashioned with his hands.
God wants you to be a Holy devout man.
You are still young and have a long way to go.
Just remember that we will always reap what we sow
So whatever you do in life always do your best.
God will never let you settle for anything less.
Jarvis you are my heart and I am always here for you.
So always make your Auntie proud in everything that you do.

Mother Dear

It has been a year since you've been gone.

Somehow we all feel like we are so alone.

We do truly miss you in each and every day.

You brought us all so much joy in each and every way.

You taught us all the things that we really needed to know.

You show us all so much and which way that we should go.

You taught us the things that we all should choose to do.

Now we proudly live our lives just to honor you.

We know that there will never be another.

That can take the place of our Dear Mother.

Here are some things that you should know. You are with
us everywhere that we go.

We carry you in our daily walk. You fashion the way that
we think and talk.

It's because of you that we are here today. You led us to
Christ and taught us to pray.

You made a great contribution to the world.

Your life was more precious than diamonds and pearls.

So we are proud to present this candlelight to you.

It symbolizes that our love is true.

You are forever embedded within our heart. Not even
death will keep us apart.

We were devastated when God called you home.
But wrapped in his arms is where you belong.
So we are not going to worry although we may cry.
For you are our Guardian Angel in the infinite sky.
Mother Dear we thank you for all that you did for us . . .

Big Cuz

The first of 28 cousins who all proclaim that
they are the best.
Big Cuz was a marine because he wouldn't settle for less.
God bless Big Cuz for his spirit is in your hands.
We all have a scheduled appointment according
to your plan.
We will all leave this world one day, when we do not know.
But there is some work that we all must do
before its time to go.
Big Cuz was so much fun in each and every way.
He always spoke his mind and said what he had to say.
He always did his things thus doing what he had to do.
There is nothing in this world that he wouldn't
do for me or you.
He was the first of many cousins and really
cherished his mother.
He always tried to be right there for his 3 loving brothers.
There was a time in his life when he really got off track.
But his love for his wife and kids brought him right back.
He always loved his family, for them
he turned his life around.
For this unselfish attitude, Big Cuz is Heaven bound.

Being a devout family man can bring you close to God.
I am glad that my big cousin Willie B stepped up and
did his part.
Big Cuz we are all tired for living is such a test.
Now you are safe in Jesus arms and
can finally get some rest.

Color Blind

The world is a better place now thanks to
Dr. Martin Luther King.
He did all he could when he was alive to make
freedom ring.
Back then it was color blind and you could not see.
I a lot of people were treated wrong all because
they weren't free.
It was white against black; the world was
shattered in pieces.
But until one day someone open their eyes to see.
He said that it was not suppose to be like this,
why right now?
I have a dream and I expect it to come true.
This world is color blind can't you see, black kids and
white kids can't even play free.
This is the day when all God children will be able to let
freedom ring, where we will love one another and
play together.
Go to school together, stay in the same house together,
and be together.
Let it ring from every village and for every hamlet.

Let it ring for every teacher who wants this dream
to come true.
And also let it ring for you.

Thank you Dr. Martin Luther King for saving the world!

Kabretta L. Brown

Face to Face

You may not know it but I am as smart as you.
What I am saying you know is true.
I stay in my place where I belong.
You capture me and destroy my home.
I have a family just like you.
Locked in your cage what am I to do?
Being stored away for you to enjoy.
I am God's creature not your earthly toy.
I am smarter that you are so leave me alone.
In my habitation you don't belong.
Your world is so full of hate.
Change it fast before it's too late.
My world has become a jungle too.
It got that way because of you.

Harm's Way

The Grim Reaper, Harm way is who I am.
For your sacred life I will steal it from the lamb.
For your mind and soul I really don't even care.
It's your sacred body that me and Hell wants to share.
Come to me so I can help you burn forever and more.
You have no idea but you are already standing at the door.
The next step that you take might be your last.
I am trained to take you ever so fast.
After I get you all is well.
I'm dragging you straight to the Gates of Hell.
My devices are plenty, your choices are few.
Step in my world, your will be through.
In order to defeat me this is what you must do.
Accept Jesus as your Savior and let him fight for you.

Angel

Look at you!
You are a star.
You illuminating beauty shine from afar.
Your inner aura is pure and clean.
Your qualifications are that of a queen.
The luxurious texture of your wavy black hair.
Seems so lovely that it's too much to bear.
Just look at your face with that adorable smile.
You have beautiful skin and an immaculate style.
Is everyone blind or is something wrong with me?
Your beauty is so impeccable that it's obvious to see.
Physical beauty is only skin deep but eternal
beauty is to the bone.
God placed you Angels in a class of your own.

You

It's easy for me to love you so it's senseless for me to say.
That my eyes look forward to seeing your face each
and every day.
My hands look forward to touching you, just to feel
your beautiful skin.
For your body is so immaculate that they know not
where to begin.
My body looks forward to touch yours; it seems
like a heavenly place.
Every time I lay beside you it puts me in a daze.
My ears look forward to hearing your voice.
Which sound so sensationally sweet.
No matter where I will know the sound for its
ultimately unique.
I don't know about my heart.
It has a mind of its own.
But right from the very start it claimed you as a home.

God Almighty

Happy Father's day to God from every one of us.
For He is the one that made us from his very own dust.
He formed us with his hands and fashioned us with style.
Then He breathed the breath of life in us and
claimed us as his child.
We are forever grateful for what he did for us.
The only thing that He wants is love, dedication and trust.
So let's give God our all for He truly deserves the best.
Besides our Heavenly Father wouldn't settle
for anything less.
He gave us living waters and pure air to breathe.
Then he adorned the earth with more beauty than eyes
could ever conceive.
Blessed be our Father for he is worthy to be praised.
For he alone blesses us even with our wicked ways.
So if this is the day for Fathers.
God created man!
Today he should get extra honors all across the land.

Happy Father's day to God Almighty

Who am I?

Who am I?

Who wants to know?

You wouldn't believe me if I told you so.

You wouldn't believe that I sit on high. And control the
world from the infinite sky.

You won't believe that I know everything. Even the
weather before the season brings.

You won't believe that I can raise the dead.

And by a little boy's lunch 5000 people were fed.

You won't believe that I turned water into wine.

And gave sight to some people who were born blind.

Who am I?

Do you really want to know? Listen closely and I will tell
you so.

Close your eyes and open your mind. Picture the ocean
that's so divine.

Picture the sand along its shore. Now come to me for I
have opened the door.

For I am like the ocean vast deep and wide.

You can never see the other side.

You will never know nor can you understand.

My infinite wisdom is too mighty for man. I am the way
the truth and the light.

Everything that I do is honorable and right.

I made the beast with eyes to and fro. Just to see you
anywhere that you go.

I AM that I AM, I am the Lamb, I am the
Father of Abraham.

Ears can never hear nor can eyes ever see the glorious
power inside of me.

Who am I?—Who wants to know?

If you are sure I will tell you so.

I am all that I appear to be I AM that I AM!

Revelation

I thank you for letting me see your face.
For within my heart it can never be erased.
Within my life you will always be.
I will love you throughout eternity.
It was unbearable for me to see you go.
You were my whole world and I love you so.
You brought joy and happiness into my life.
I was always delighted just being your wife.
We have no control over God's plan.
Our present, past and future is in his hands.
When you love someone from the depth of your heart.
Not even death will keep you apart.
I watched you fall asleep, I watched you awake.
I use to inhale every breath that you take.
I am right by your side everywhere that you go. Lisa my
dear I still love you so.
Life is a mystery in your world and mines
Sometimes true love can cross the line.
So don't be afraid to call my name.
And please don't feel like you are to blame.

I know that you will never let me go.

Be happy live life and go with the flow.

You don't have to worry and you don't have to cry.

I am your guardian Angel in the infinite sky.

True love never ends, it transcends.

I Believe

Yes I am Kabrina and I do believe.

Oh yeah I believe that I can achieve.

You left me alone and thought that I was gone.

But it seems that you were very wrong.

Look at me yes I am back and you better believe I'm taking
up the slack.

Yes I believe that I can make it.

And I know that you can't take it.

You tried to put me down but guess what?

I'm back in town.

I am going to school to make all A's.

And I will make myself have better days.

You put me down, thought that I was a clown.

But I am back and you can bet that I will be around.

Kabrina Brown

Love

Love is something that comes from deep inside.
Love is a feeling that you just can't hide.
When two people are in love it comes from the heart.
When two people come together it is a good start.
Loving someone is a very responsible bond.
When you love someone it's not just for fun.
Love can be intimidating, love can be discriminating.
Love can be everything except for hating.
When you love someone you share and you care.
And no matter what the case you will always be there.

Kabrina Brown

Drug-Free

Drug free is the best way to be.

Who me?

I am free to be the best that I can be.

Put drugs to the side, let's take a ride.

I must warn you that it's a dangerous drive.

It's your duty to live, you be the guide.

Whatever you do don't go inside.

Look there is the leader passing around a needle.

They all are trying to be a cheater.

There goes an old man trying to sell a heater.

Only to get beat down by the leader.

Look at that family living in a ten.

Trying to make a dollar out of fifteen cent.

Drugs got their mother, now the children suffer.

Buying the drugs from her brother.

Come on hurry there is more to see.

Why can't you be just like me?

Completely Drug-Free

Kabrina Brown

Life

The game of life is an over-rated strife.
Everything that we do is a sacrifice.
You have to follow rules and directions
everywhere that you go.
These are the things that we should already know.
No one was asked to be here and no one
will be asked to leave.
But we must set some goals that we would like to achieve.
Sometime life can be good, sometimes life can be bad.
Sometimes it can be happy and sometimes it can be bad.
You have to face reality to make a brighter community.
You must make a choice to choose right from wrong.
And most of all we must get along.
There is one thing that is always best.
Try God and put him to a test.

Kabrina Brown

The Lord

The lord is good to me in so many ways.
He makes me feel worthwhile on my bad days.
He wakes me up every morning just to see the light.
He lets me know that his spirit is right.
He shows me how much he care as he share.
Then tell me that he'll always be there.
He is always so forgiving.
And show me that love is the purpose for living.
He tells me to pray to make my trouble go away.
Then he shows me a brighter day.
Everybody thinks that we are odd.
But they do not know that we are the Children of God.
Let's keep doing right instead of wrong.
Then life won't seem like a seem old song.
Next time you feel like things are a little too hard.
Fall on your knees and praise the Lord.

Mother

Mother is your title and your claim to fame
By the Blessing of giving birth you were given that
name.

M—Is for mighty as in a woman giving birth
Submitting to God's will by populating
The earth
O—Is for officer being that you are the
head of my life.
Being totally immune to controversy and strife.

T—Is for teacher for all learning starts with you. You
Taught me everything and was always true

H—Stands for hero which you will always
be to me. You
Continually gave me encouragement then set me free.

E—Is for everlasting which my love for you
will always be.
I continually thank God for giving you to me.

R—Is for your royalty for you will always
be my queen.
Within my world you are everything

You are already a legend, a great title to behold.
To me you are more precious than diamonds and
gold.

Mattie

A mighty mother is who you are.

You are indeed my shining star.

Dear Mother there is something that I'd like you to know.

You're embedded in my soul wherever you go.

I feel you in my heart and in the things that I do.

The success that I have attained is all because of you.

Taller than the mountains, deeper than the sea.

My love for you runs continually.

I thank God for the wisdom that you ultimately behold.

And your love for me will never get cold.

I thank God for the greatest Mom of all.

I hope that I can always answer your call.

I love you more than words can say.

And I am cherishing you more dearly on this Blessed
Mother's day.

Mother I thank God for you

Happy Mother's Day

James Jr.

Our Momma

This is the only poem that I never wanted to write.
But I knew that a call would come would come one night.
Yes I knew that she would leave us one day.
And there would be nothing that we could say.
But we can say with pride that there was no other,
Stronger Black Woman than our Mother.
Momma had 10 children at the age of 25.
All of us are gifted and wise.
Momma raised us by herself, yes all alone.
Momma guided, protected and gave us a home.
We rarely got what we wanted, but she fulfilled all our needs.
Momma fed us God's word thus planting the seed.
Momma completed her job a long time ago.
From the oldest to the baby, she helped us to grow.
Our Mother was blessed to live a very full life.
Momma didn't tolerate with controversy and strife.
Momma said what she meant and meant what she said.
Back in her days she painted the town red.
We'll never forget the good times that we had.
Which somehow always outweighed the bad.
Momma will suffer no more and have no more pain.
Our mother didn't lose, In fact she gained.

Momma has earned her crown that's solid in gold.

Unto our God she has committed her soul.

Her troubles of this world are over and gone.

Our sweet wonderful Mother has finally gone home.

For we'll grow stronger and stick together.

For momma taught us to be stronger than leather.

Momma taught us well so let's do our best.

For we know that Momma wouldn't settle for less.

So let us not worry and try not to cry.

For Momma is with God in the infinite sky.

God take care of our Momma . . .

Momma we'll always love you . . .

Debra, Belinda, Dorothy, James, Anthony, Angela, Joel,

Johnny, Jackie &Charles